# APPRENTICED TO MAGIC
# &
# MAGIC AND THE QABALAH

Two classic works from the pen of the late W. E. Butler.

# APPRENTICED TO MAGIC
## AND
# MAGIC & THE QABALAH

## W. E. BUTLER

Introduced by
Dolores Ashcroft-Nowicki

THE AQUARIAN PRESS

*Apprenticed to Magic* first published 1962
*Magic and the Qabalah* first published 1964
This compilation volume published 1990

© THE AQUARIAN PRESS 1978, 1981

British Library Cataloguing in Publication Data

Butler, W.E. (Walter Ernest), *1898–1978*
Apprenticed to magic; and, Magic & the qabalah.
1. Paranormal phenomena
I. Title
133

ISBN 0-85030-961-1

*The Aquarian Press is part of the Thorsons Publishing Group, Wellingborough, Northamptonshire, NN8 2RQ, England*

Typeset by Harper Phototypesetters Ltd., Northampton, England

Printed in Great Britain by Hartnolls Ltd, Bodmin, Cornwall

1  3  5  7  9  10  8  6  4  2

# CONTENTS

# PREFACE

LITTLE need be written as a preface to this book. Following my usual custom, I have written to illumine as well as to instruct, and my writing is aimed at the deeper levels of the minds of my readers. How far I may succeed in this depends upon many factors, some of which are outside my conscious control. I can only send the book forth upon its mission and trust that it may help some of its readers to understand a little more of the wonderful philosophy of the Qabalah.

Again I have to thank my patient amanuensis, Mrs Hilda Eastburn, for her help in the preparation and typing of the manuscript of the book. Under somewhat difficult conditions she has been of the greatest help to me in its initial production.

I have also to acknowledge with gratitude advice and help given to me by the Warden of the Society of the Inner Light.

Finally, I would thank all those readers of my earlier books who have written to me. May this book prove worthy of its dedication to those who were true exponents of the philosophy outlined therein, and to whom I owe far more than I can ever say.

W. E. Butler
Southampton, 1963

# INTRODUCTION

WHEN the time comes to look back upon the twentieth century it will be known for many things, not the least of which will be the widespread resurgence of occult theory and practice. In the last 25 years it has grown into a multimillion-pound industry that is still growing, despite all the efforts of fundamentalist Christianity to undermine it. There have been certain men and women who have been in the forefront of the long battle to gain acceptance and recognition for their beliefs and the way has not been an easy one. A. E. Waite, Florence Farr, W. B. Yeats, Aleister Crowley (who, though many despise the man and his actions, it must be admitted has his place in this roll call), McGregor Mathers, Brodie Innes, Dion Fortune, C. R. S. Seymour, Christine Hartley, Paul Case, Israel Regardie, and a man whose work spanned 60 years of his life, W. E. Butler.

In a crowd you would not have noticed him unless possessed of trained psychic abilities, then you would have noted the extended aura and the sigil of the Teacher. He was neither tall nor distinguished in looks, but once in his company you became aware of the innate greatness of the man. There was a warmth and a genuine desire to reach out and touch the heart of those he taught. He was in all things thorough and dedicated, not least in the way he prepared those who were to follow him.

Those of us who were privileged to learn from this man will never forget him; our lives were changed at the first meeting, and when we meet we exchange stories and anecdotes about our times with him. He still affects our lives and through us the lives of those who come after and who will never know the man, only his teachings.

The book you hold in your hand contains his own view of magic and its application to everyday life. He believed, fervently, that it should permeate one's whole life, not shut away to be brought out on special days only and seen as something darkly mysterious and intended only for "initiates". For Ernest Butler magic was a way of life and of living; his writings reflect that belief and, although his prose may seem old-fashioned to those of you used to a more modern style, understand that he wrote from the viewpoint of another, older, and less frenetic generation. It is 11 years since his death, but what he has to say, his methods of teaching and his wisdom still have a place in the lives of those who step onto the Path of the Mysteries.

*Apprenticed to Magic* is rather different to most books on the subject in that it is written in the first person singular. It takes the form of a teacher's letters and instructions to his student and as such it is quite unique. Ernest Butler's personal teaching style comes through very strongly and anyone who has had the opportunity to listen to the few taped lectures that he made will recognize the delivery and the phraseology. Step-by-step the apprentice is taken through a series of lessons, with mistakes noticed and commented upon and due praise given. The book is ideal for those who as yet have not made a commitment but which to understand more magical training before doing so.

*Magic and the Qabalah* was Ernest's last major book, and though he wrote articles for many years after this all his time was given to directing the correspondence course that still exists today. It is a compact text book that set forth the basics of the Qabalah and matches it with the practice of the Western Mystery Tradition. It is not as well known as his other books and that is a pity since it deserves more than a cursory glance. Since it was written in 1964 there have been many other books written on the same subject, but *Magic and the Qabalah* offers Ernest Butler's own unique way of looking at — and what is more to the point — teaching it.

Ernest spent a long time in India during his younger days and he made full use of what he learned there, something that makes this edition close to being a bridge between Eastern and Western philosophy. This was a man who never decried other people's religions but simply saw them as fellow travellers on the Path. For myself, I am happy to see his books reprinted again and to know that another generation of seekers will be able to read and assimilate his gentle wisdom. Cheiron we called him, a name in which he delighted, a name he richly deserved.

Dolores Ashcroft-Nowicki
Jersey, November 1989

# APPRENTICED TO MAGIC

# CHAPTER I

## "WELL MET"

YOU wish to tread High Magic's Way.

There are many questions which arise in my mind as I read your letter. You seem to be sincere in your desire, but before I can accept you for training, I want to clear up some of the points which are raised by your application. First of all, I think it will be helpful to us both if we find out how far we are speaking the same language.

Of course, we are both using our English tongue, but I wonder whether you realize how easy it is for one person to fail entirely when seeking to impart the significance of his or her ideas to another? The *methods* of communication now in use are exceedingly efficient, but, and here is the real point at issue, are the ideas communicated in their fullness, and is the communication free from distortion? This is quite another question, and it is of the utmost importance that we should so use our methods of communication that the ideas which we wish to convey may be received without distortion by those whom we are addressing.

I have certain teaching, certain ideas and instructions, which I must convey to you should you become my "apprentice". But what pre-conceived ideas have you on these matters?

The other day a friend of long standing accused me of putting to-gether a lot of occult odds and ends and of calling the resultant mix-ture "magic". All my efforts to alter this misconception have failed, and for a very sufficient reason. *His* conception of "magic" is one which does not cover the vast system of graded instruction and prac-tice which is the heritage of the initiates of the Western Mysteries. In these Mysteries I was trained, and it is with them alone that I am concerned.

If you desire to learn of wonderful oriental magic, of systems of yoga which will enable you to perform the wonders which the popular mind associates with yoga, then I am afraid you must look elsewhere. There is a great deal of nonsense abroad in the west regarding the marvels of the east. Some forms of Hatha Yoga have been popular-ized and adapted as physical training methods, and almost every week we read in the popular press of some actress, or "deb", or busi-ness man having restored health by standing on her (or his) head, or by practising *pranayama*.

Many years ago I studied these things in India with a small group of Hindus who were experts in various forms of yoga, and I know what a wonderful thing yoga is. However, that which the west is pleased to term yoga, is but a small part of the real thing. But, and this is the point I want to impress upon you, eastern yoga is designed for eastern bodies and conditions, and except in its most elementary forms it is unsuitable for western bodies. In addition to this the racial psychology of the east differs from that of the west, and instructions which can be readily accepted by eastern pupils would arouse intense psychological resistances in the minds of those western students who tried to carry them out. I am not trying to belittle the eastern systems, I know their value, but I am convinced that the methods which have been evolved by the Western Tradition for use by western people, are the best *for us*. "To every man his own Master, and who art thou to judge another's servant? To his own Master he stands or falls."

What is your reaction to this point of view? If you become my apprentice you will have to follow the western methods; also, and this is where trouble usually arises, you will have to give your word of honour that you will not mix the techniques; that is, you will not introduce snippets of other methods into the exercises which will be given to you.

Perhaps you have had the idea, common to many people, that magic is something of eastern origin, and you may wish to ask me what *I* consider it to be? This is a legitimate question, and I will try to answer it. You say you have read my books. In both of these I have defined "magic", in the words of one of my own teachers, as, "The art of effecting changes in consciousness at will". I wonder if I was sufficiently clear in my explanation of this definition? It seems that I was not, for I have had letters from several people who seemed to feel that it was rather vague. Why should a change of consciousness, whether willed or unwilled, have such power that its manifestations are known by the ancient and venerable name of "magic"? As you will learn (if I accept you for training) all the operations of magic are based upon an essential unity which exists between man, who is known as the "microcosmos", the little universe, and the external universe, the "macrocosmos". This unity has always existed since manifestation first began, but the normal waking consciousness possesses not the keys to its own inner kingdom. Only in times of overwhelming stress, or in certain abnormal conditions of the mind or body, do the latent powers of the magical man within manifest themselves. Deep within that inner kingdom is the "ground" where the powers of the outer universe make contact with the inner universe of man. Shift the focus of consciousness and these powers and energies manifest themselves through the channel of the human personality.

So all magic starts from within, and all the paraphernalia of ceremonial and ritual are aids whereby the inner powers may be summoned forth. In our Western Tradition these things will be taught to you in a special way, and by an age-old technique. If you follow this technique in its entirety, then at a certain stage the key to your own inner kingdom will be placed in your hand, and you will be able to change the gears of consciousness at will. How you use this power will depend entirely upon yourself, but believe me, if you abuse the power you gain, then you will indeed live to rue it. This is not a matter of theory on my part. I am not retailing secondhand stories to you. I have myself seen, in actual operation, the consequences of such abuse of power, and the spectacle was not one to encourage me to make that mistake.

Of course, it is possible that you may make mistakes; all apprentices in every field of activity do make mistakes. It is by these mistakes that they learn their craft, since the discipline involved in rectifying them perfects the craftsmen. But such mistakes are understood, and the worst consequences are neutralized by those under whom they are being trained.

This brings me to the next point which I want to discuss with you. You have asked me to train you in High Magic's Way. Why do you wish to be trained? What is your real motive. Do not make the mistake of thinking that this can be answered without a good deal of careful thought. You see, there are often motives which arise from the depths of our consciousness and which have not been decided upon by the normal waking mind. Some of these are very real and very good reasons; others are unreal and irrational, and are the products of some buried mental-emotional "complex", as the psychologists call it.

There is a word which is used in this connection, it is "vocation"; a real and definite "call" or urge which wells up from within, and which will, against seemingly tremendous odds, force the personality to follow a certain line of work. This then, is an urge of the inner self, and of it we may say, in the words of the Grail poem, "If thou hast by Him been bidden, from thee the truth will not stay hidden."

The test of these inner impulses is whether they persist through all kinds of outer difficulty, and also whether they influence us towards a balanced state of mind. The irrational impulses towards the study of magic are usually compensations, i.e., the subconscious self feels that the powers gained by magical art will compensate for certain inferiorities which are deeply resented by a level of the mind which does no *reason*, but simply *feels*.

There are, of course, quite good motives for the study and practice of magic, quite apart from the question of vocation. It is a worthy motive to search for truth, *if the results of that search are going to be used in service.* "I desire to know in order to serve," is the motive which admits to the Mysteries. As you will see, we are touching upon the moral order of things, and, this I must impress upon you: in the mysteries this moral standard is enforced most rigidly, for the power which is gained by this training can be used for good or evil purposes. It is for this reason that this pledge is asked of you at the beginning of your training. Remember, however, that at every stage of your magical career the temptation to misuse these powers for your own personal ends will recur. Never think that you will be free from such temptation. You can and will be aided to fight against it, but the temptation itself will come. This may sound rather grim, but it must be made clear, even though it may scare you away.

There is yet another thing that I must point out. We have been thinking of you as being accepted or rejected as my apprentice. This is true, but only in so far as I am allowed to use my own discretion as to whom I may accept for training. But I, too, am "a man under authority", and the senior craftsman under whom I work has the deciding voice in this matter. The brotherhood is affected by the entrance of all admitted, and the brethren have a right to be considered. So, even if I do accept you for training, that acceptance must be ratified by my own chief before we can begin your apprenticeship.

Now think carefully over all that I have written. Give it your concentrated attention, and look yourself squarely in the face. Do not try to deceive yourself, but answer the questions I have suggested. If your self-examination leads you to believe that you both wish and are able to take part in the Great Work and to tread High Magic's Way, then let me know. With the approval of my chief we will then begin our work which is nothing less than the breaking down and rebuilding of your own soul. I hope you will pass the test and that we shall work together.

# CHAPTER II

## "APPLICATION ACCEPTED"

I HAVE received your letter and have submitted it to my chief who has agreed, that if it is my wish, I may accept you as my apprentice in Art Magic. May our joint efforts be to the greater glory of God, and to the service of man. You will note that I was told I might take you as my apprentice *if I so wished.* Herein lies an important point, for from this time onwards, until our association ceases, I am responsible for you in a very real sense. Should you break the rules, then I, because I am your teacher, must share the responsibility. It is the knowledge of this binding liability and obligation which makes us so very careful before accepting anyone for training.

Let me mention something else. It is the general idea that, in the relationship between the teacher and pupil, the main thing is that the pupil receives certain *teaching*. This, however, is only a part of the truth so far as magical instruction is concerned. Instruction is given in such a way that it will really *educate*. This process of drawing out the ideas of the pupil (for that is what education really is) means that a very strong link is built up between teacher and pupil. This is the second factor. But there is another relationship which builds up. This is due to a change in the teacher's personality because of the interaction of the pupil's personality with his own. There is a steady exchange, a kind of psychic osmosis which affects both. This is true of ordinary psycho-analytical treatment, but it is much more definite in occult and magical training.

It may be that you will object to this idea and tell me that as we are not meeting physically, such a rapport cannot be established. If you make this objection you will be wrong, for such a link can be set up over any distance, since in its essence it is telepathic. Get out of your head the idea that telepathy has anything to do with distance. All our knowledge of it (and the recorded experience which is stored in the esoteric archives, is far more extensive than the average member of the Society for Psychical Research ever realizes) goes to prove that bodily absence is no bar to its operation between two or more people.

There *are* certain forces which do depend upon the physical contact, or at least proximity, of those concerned; but this peculiar rapport between pupil and teacher is not limited by any such spatial circumstance. Remember, then, that in this magical apprenticeship there will be built up between us a very real link. Moreover this link can operate for our mutual benefit or for our mutual discomfort and loss.

We may use a metaphor and say that between us is established a line of light. Indeed, to the average psychic, this is what the link may seem to be, and as we always tend to think in space-time images, there is no reason why you should not visualize in this manner the psychic tie which will hold us together during your apprenticeship. At a certain stage towards the end of your training this link will be deliberately modified, in order that you may be able to stand on your own feet and in no way be dependent upon me. The whole aim of magical training is to integrate the personality, so that in all your mundane and supermundane affairs you will display a balanced and controlled mind. In the meantime, as I have said, this psychic thread will link us together, and, as I shall show you at a later stage of your training, it can be of great assistance to us both.

Now let us start to clear the ground in order that we may commence our work in the correct way. This means that we must first study the conditions under which you must train. I am sure you have either heard of, or met, budding authors who are of the hot-house type. They must have their own particular room, their own chair, their special pen, and so on. Without these they simply cannot do any work. It is very helpful, if at the outset of your magical training you can provide yourself with congenial surroundings, but they are not necessary. They can, in fact, become virtual fetters, since it is possible to form a mental habit of relying upon them to such a degree, that as in the cases to which I have referred, it is found impossible to work without them.

The whole aim of this training is to give you an integrated personality; a personality no longer at the mercy of its surroundings. It is important therefore, that independence of environment is acquired as soon as possible. In my own case, when I first began my magical training at the beginning of the First World War, I was in lodgings. I had precious little time, or opportunity, to establish the conditions I considered desirable. The result was that my progress was much slower than it might have been, but I learnt to meditate and to do other mental work under very difficult conditions. My own teacher used to say that proficiency was not to be hoped for until it was possible to meditate successfully while seated in the middle of Waterloo Station. This may sound difficult, but he was right. So the fact that you are not able to establish your own special conditions, need not deter you from making a start on your training.

I think I ought to make one more point quite clear before we pass on to other matters. Although meditating in the atmosphere of Waterloo Railway Station is possible, this does not imply that I am suggesting that you should attempt any purely *psychic* work under such conditions. "Opening-up" to psychic influences in the early days of training is inadvisable. When you are stabilized and integrated, you will be able to "open up" and "close down" at will, but in the beginning you must comply with the instructions you are given, and indiscriminate psychic "sensing" will not be one of them.

We will assume that you have to use your bedroom as your meditation centre. Should you be more fortunate, I will give you the instructions for building up your own special conditions, but these must be temporary aids, not permanent crutches. All you need is the room and a reasonable amount of privacy. But you must exercise a certain amount of discrimination. If you are stridently insistent upon everyone being quiet during your meditation period, you may very possibly evoke from those around you that perverse little mental imp which is to be found in the best of us, and quite a lot of unnecessary noise will, quite unconsciously, be produced. In any case, the neighbour's dog will not be amenable to your requests or commands!

In the beginning, therefore, you will have to struggle to keep going on your meditations and progress will not seem very good. All the time, however, you will be building up an interior mental state which will make you independent of outer conditions. As a matter of fact, this principle is involved in the whole of your training, for, as you become proficient in the magical work, you learn to dispense with the outer rites and ceremonies, and to work entirely within your own integrated personality, using the inner powers which your magical training has developed. So, also, in the difficulties which may come your way, see always the instruments which, if you use them aright, will prove to be helps, not hindrances, on your path.

The next point with which I want to deal is the question of "postures". You have probably read about the wonderful attitudes in which some eastern yogis meditate. The most usual of these is known as *padmasana*, or "The Lotus Posture", but this is not usually possible for Europeans, unless they have either trained consistently from childhood, or have naturally loose ligaments. It is helpful if you can use such a posture, but it is not essential. There are many of these bodily positions, but we in the western schools use only those which are adapted for use with the western body. There is no sense in meditating successfully in the lotus position if you break the small bones of the foot in the process.

For the purposes of your meditation exercise you will need for the present at least, only a fairly comfortable chair. If you are trying to control and direct the mind into new channels, it is somewhat foolish to give it unnecessary distractions due to bodily discomfort. At the same time remember that in these exercises the mind must be alert, and this is not always possible if you have too comfortable a chair. The ideal chair to use is, as a matter of fact, a somewhat hard, wooden one, an armchair for preference. An "easy chair" is the last kind you should use.

The only other thing you now need for your work is a good exercise book in which to record the results of your meditations. It may be helpful, but it is not essential, for you to have some particular symbolic picture or image which can be placed before you as a reminder of your work. When using these pictures or figures as focusing points, you should err on the side of austerity. Have only one or two; the multiplication of such aids to meditation is more likely to hinder than to help. I remember preaching in a church where the pulpit was adorned with six crosses of varying material, ranging from perspex to brass. Greatly though I revere this symbol, I found its unnecessary multiplication distracting rather than helpful.

If you are so situated that you cannot put aside a room for your meditation work here is a very helpful procedure you can adopt. Put your symbolic picture in a small frame that will stand on the table, and have made for it a cover which can be slipped over it when you have finished your meditations. Keep your picture or symbolic image locked away with your magical diary; never leave them lying about.

Here you must use your discretion. Your wife may feel that she should know what you are doing, and if you are too secretive she may take steps to register her disapproval. It is far better, then, for you to let her see these things if she wishes, especially at the beginning of your training. If she is interested and desires to help you in the work, she will not take undue advantage of the privilege. If, on the other hand, she disapproves of the whole business, the permission to see the "tools" of your work may help to allay any doubts she may have. (The same thing applies, of course, to women students whose husbands may, or may not, approve of their interest in these matters, though in these days men do not, as a rule, actively interfere with the occupations of their womenfolk.) In any case, this is a matter with which you must deal as soon as possible. Discuss it with your wife, and see how far she is prepared to help you along this line.

Another point: so many people feel that the "atmosphere" they desire for their meditation can be established by the use of incense.

This is true, but there are many different kinds of incense, and not all are suitable for your work. In fact, there are some varieties which are very definitely taboo as far as this work is concerned. The main effect of the usual kinds of incense employed is to associate the meditation with the scent of the incense smoke in such a way that whenever the incense is burning, it will recall the meditation to mind. It has also a certain "psychic" effect with which I will deal at a later date.

Unfortunately, incense has a habit of advertising its presence, and a very little can go a very long way. If you have a room set apart for your work, then this will enable you to use incense without any trouble, but if you must use a room which is also used by others, then I would advise you to do without incense. It is not vitally necessary, and it is better for you to do without it, rather than to cause needless antagonism by insisting upon permeating the whole house with its fragrance. Apart from this, the mingled aroma of incense and break- fast bacon is not particularly helpful to either student or cook. Al- though you are entitled to your own point of view, you are *not* en- titled to carry it out in such a way as to cause discomfort to others with whom you are linked. Any such occult selfishness would hinder rather than help you.

Now for a most important instruction. It is essential that you should separate your meditation from your ordinary mundane work. I know this will raise some queries in your mind. Surely you will say, it is good to go out to the workaday world with the mental stimulus of the work done in meditation? Yes, I agree it is very helpful to do this, and if you have performed your meditation correctly, then you will have that keynote vibrating in the depths of your mind. It will not be necessary for you consciously to keep trying to put on the mask of the particular virtue you may have used as the subject of your meditation.

However, you, in your mental work, will have been directing your thoughts and personal energies along what we term "inner lines", and it is very necessary that when the work on these lines is done, you should revert to the outer world and its concerns. "We cannot at the shrine remain," says a line of a hymn, and indeed, it would not be good for the majority of us to do so. There are those who are called to a purely contemplative life, but they are few. So, when you finish your meditation, you must "close down", that is you must bring back your attention to the material world. If you go out from your mental work in a confused condition, then you will have trouble sooner or later. In any case your discipline is clear: *you must not do this*, but I want you to understand why we are so insistent on this particular point. When you begin to meditate you dissociate yourself from outer things in order that you may deal with the inner, subjective world. It is imperative that when the inner work is done you should re-associate yourself with that outer world in which you have to work. If you neglect this, then there will come about a gradual disco-ordination in your mind, and it will become more and more difficult for you to take up the heat and burden of the day. You will tend to, drift into an escapism which, instead of improving your personality, will cause you to become increasingly inefficient in both worlds. You may have thought that this insistence upon the return to normal was exaggerated, but I trust you will now see our reasons for it.

For the moment I will not give you any more detailed instructions, as I want you to study carefully what has already been given. You are beginning a piece of work which will have far-reaching effects, and I want you to feel sure that it is a task which you are determined to follow through to the end. You will find that the routine becomes tedious, and you may feel inclined to cavil at what appears, in the early stages at least, to be without any apparent result. I say "in the early stages", but this is not really correct. At the start of your work you will most probably have some very definite results, but as you go on you will find that these initial experiences seem to fade away, and you have to follow a dull routine which seems neither exciting nor helpful. It is then that you will find that the scripture is very true: "It is the little foxes that spoil the vines"; they can squeeze through the hedge where the bigger ones would fail. So, as you set off on your magical career, you must fence against the foxes, and feel that the vineyard of your personality is secure. But with the discipline and the exercises being carried out day by day, you may insensibly begin to allow the little foxes of boredom and impatience, to mention only two, to get through the fence. We who have essayed this path have all gone through this phase. With some it is more apparent than with others, but in one way or another it affects us all.

There is a certain rhythm in this work. A time of success and illumination is followed by a period of "dryness" and a descent into the Valley of Humiliation. Then we have to plod along until we begin to see once more the light ahead. All who venture out into these hidden ways of the mind have experienced this swing of the mental pendulum and this applies in the same way to those who follow the path of the mystic. They, like those of us who tread the magical way, find that this comes to them too. Indeed, the term "dryness" which I have just used, comes from the terminology of the mystics.

Think over what I have told you. Re-read it and try to fix it firmly in your mind. Although these first instructions may seem commonplace, they contain basic truths, and are an essential part of the foundation which you must build in yourself, my apprentice.

Let me know whether you need any more initial instruction on these points before we go any further. Do not be afraid to ask any questions which arise from what I have told you. In our school of training we value the questioning mind, providing it carries out the instructions given.

Let me know also whether it *is* possible for you to have a separate room for your work. In the next instructions I shall give you the basic exercises in magical meditation, and you will then be able to make a definite start.

# CHAPTER III

# FIRST EXERCISES

I GATHER from your letter that you have discussed with your wife the question of a place for meditation, and have reached a satisfactory arrangement. You tell me that you will be able to have a small room reserved for your work. This is good news, although, as I told you, such good conditions should never be allowed to cause you to rely too much upon them.

Furnish your meditation room simply. Have in it only the necessary chair and table. On the table you may place a vase of fresh flowers, together with whatever picture or image you may wish to use as a focusing point. If you decide to use incense, then employ a good type of incense stick; there are many kinds of incense as I told you, but this is probably the best for general work. You will need some form of holder in which to burn the incense stick, but I ask you not to use one of these made in the form of the Lord Buddha. So many people do use them, but it is due, in the main, to lack of imagination. Would you, as a Christian, feel entirely comfortable if you found an Oriental friend using a crucifix as an incense burner? For many millions of people the Lord Gautama Buddha is their great teacher and for that reason, if for no other, you should refrain from using such a thing. Sometimes one finds such a brass figure which, although it is often taken for an image of the Buddha, is really one of the god of luck, Chenresi. But even this should not be used. You are following the *Western* path.

I daresay you will be wondering what exercises you will receive, and what disciplines you must accept. For the present I am going to give you the basic exercises, and, as I warned you before, they may become very dull and boring. However, they are fundamental, and must be carried out. Without the proficiency you will gain in them, your further meditation would be erratic, so persevere with them and you will begin to appreciate their value. However, before I enter a description of the first exercise, I want to raise certain points with regard to your training.

First of all, I want you to be perfectly sure in your mind of the obligations which you have undertaken by entering our school. The most important thing to remember in this connection is that you are not under any vow of personal obedience to anyone in the school, whether it be to myself or to my superiors. At the same time you *are* under obedience to the "Rule" of the Fraternity, as are we all. It is a *system of training* with which we are dealing, not with any obedience to personalities as such. Here, of course, commonsense is needed. We who have been trained in this school very naturally think our system is a good one; but you, without such experience may feel somewhat apprehensive. So let me assure you that in this school of esoteric training you will never be asked to do anything which conflicts with your ethical code. By this I do not mean that you will be at liberty to modify the instructions and disciplines which you will receive, in order to fit them into some narrower denominational scheme. But Christian and non-Christian alike can subscribe to the summary of religious duty which is contained in the quotation which Jesus made from the Hebrew teachings: "Thou shalt love the Lord thy God with all thy heart, with all thy mind, and with all thy soul and with all thy strength; and thy neighbour as thyself." It is in the light of this summary of the divine law that you are to judge the teachings you will receive.

You may, of course, feel that if you raise any objections, even though they are perfectly sincere, you will be regarded as a nuisance and thereby be prevented from going forward. You may rest assured that there is no question of being penalized for objecting to certain points in the teaching. But since in the very nature of the training you are not yet in a position to judge with knowledge, it seems to me that you will do well to study carefully the instructions *before* raising objections. In any case, it will save me quite an amount of unnecessary work!

Following on this, I want to deal with another point which is really important. It is the question of your relationship with others and the effect which your new work will have upon them. For you must always remember that you have no right to attempt to evade your responsibilities in order to undergo this training. You have taken certain tasks upon yourself, you have linked yourself with others, and all these things are conditioning factors which you must take into account.

At the same time, however, you must remember that though you have a duty to your neighbour, to love him as yourself, you also have a duty to love yourself as you love your neighbour. If your neighbour has a right to mental freedom and "elbow room", so have you. Perhaps the majority, or a good proportion at any rate, of those who come to us for training forget this, and the first trials of the path are of their own making. You must, therefore, come to a definite understanding with those who are near to you. It must be made clear that you intend to follow this discipline, and that this will call for some co-operation from them. At the same time, you must scrupulously consider *your* duty in the matter. If in any way whatsoever you make of these disciplines an excuse to neglect your home, your wife, or your children, then, although technically you may be following the discipline as far as the letter of it goes, you will in effect be breaking it in the spirit, which is a much more serious matter.

At the same time, it is possible to overload your home duties with such a thick top-dressing of sentimentality that you allow yourself to be deflected from your purpose, and your power to follow out the disciplines to be hindered very considerably. This does not make for good relations; it leads to resentfulness on the one hand and self-righteousness on the other, reactions which are neither constructive nor helpful.

If you insist on a period of privacy for the performance of your meditation, then you must see to it that no one suffers because of it. Also, and this is important, those around you must be able to see that as far as your manifest character is concerned, the result of such training is good. It is a very difficult point, but unless it is tackled right at the start, it will continue to give you trouble.

Now for the first exercise, which is known as the "Reverse Meditation". It seems so simple that many apprentices tend to neglect it, but in this they make a great mistake. Eventually they have to come back to it. I want you to write down the instruction for yourself as I give it here, then every night without fail, you must carry out the exercise and note the results as you get them.

Each night, when you are in bed, go over the events of the day *in reverse*; that is, start with the last thing you did or said, then go back to the last but one, and so on until you arrive at the first thoughts and actions of the day. As you recall each event, consider it impartially, and regard it as if it were an entirely impersonal record. Consider separately the results of each action, thought, or word, and then try to see why these thoughts and emotions were the cause of particular effects. When you feel that you have done this successfully, pass on to the event before this and evaluate it in the same way. Continue in this manner to go backwards as far as you can to the beginning of the day.

This reverse meditation is very important. First of all, it helps to modify the usual habit of the mind to think in a time-sequence of past, present, and future. This normal thinking works very well in this three-dimensional physical world, but when you begin to open up the higher consciousness you will perceive that it has its limitations. It is then that you will appreciate this exercise. The second point is. that, by first observing the end-result and then working backwards, you will find it much harder to make the usual excuses for your conduct. This tends to check some of the activity of what is known in psychology, as the "false ego". As the destruction of this false ego is part of the process of magical training, you will see why this exercise is so valuable. Incidentally, do not be discouraged if you fall asleep long before you have reached the first event of the day. The false ego will do all it can to prevent you following out the exercise.

For the present, it is not necessary for you to go into detail in your record. But it is very necessary that you should keep such a record. As you progress in your training, you will find that the habit of recording *all* results obtained will be of the greatest help to you, and you will then appreciate its value more fully.

Unlike most diaries, this one is not to be used to bolster up your own false ego. It is, instead, a very efficient method of building up an automatic habit of careful and logical thought and action. Linked with the reverse meditation are the "Salutes". These are given at certain times of the day, and they serve two purposes. First of all, they train the "time-sense", that subconscious clock which enables us to gauge the passage of time. It is very necessary that we should keep our feet on the earth even though we are dealing with metaphysical things. In fact, it is just because we *are* dealing with these things, that we, more than most people, should have our material affairs under control. I know that it is customary in certain "occult" movements to be "unworldly"; to affect to despise the "material", and to exalt the "spiritual". Perhaps you have also thought in this way? If so, you will find, as you proceed in your training, that we in this school regard such opinions entirely erroneous.

I have said that the Salutes serve yet another purpose. This is to bring about a state of "Recollection". By this we mean that it is essential to turn our minds at stated times towards that greater Life which pervades the whole universe, and in which we live and move and have our being. Never mind about any theological ideas you may have about that Life. Just regard It as the power which sustains and orders all manifestation.

Now here are the three daily Salutes:

**Morning.** Hail to Thee, the Eternal Spiritual Sun,
whose visible Symbol now rises in the Heavens.
Hail unto Thee from the Abodes of Morning.

**Noon.**     Hail to Thee, the Eternal Spiritual Sun,
              whose visible Symbol stands now in High Heaven.
              Hail unto Thee from the Abodes of the Noonday.

**Evening**.  Hail to Thee, the Eternal Spiritual Sun,
              whose visible Symbol sets now in the Heavens.
              Hail unto Thee from the Abodes of the Evening.

I enclose a specimen page of a magical Diary, so that you may see how it is to be used. At the end of each month it should be returned to me and I will check it before sending it back to you. In the diary, record the results you obtain with the Reverse Meditation, with the Salutes and with the meditation subject which I shall set you each month. Do not try to "explain" why you failed on any particular day; just record the fact that you *did* fail. You may insert such an observation as "prevented by illness" or "disturbed by dog barking" or "unexpected visitors". But do not let these entries degenerate into *excuses*. I am sure you will see what I mean.

There will be one meditation subject for the month, and you must deal with that only during that particular period. I expect you will think that long before the end of a week you will have exhausted the subject given you for a month's meditation.

Let me tell you a story which I believe is literally true. It may help you in this matter. It is recorded of a famous naturalist that a certain young man became his pupil, as you have become mine. On his first day with the great man, he was given a very simple job. "I want you to study this fish, and write down all you can about it." The naturalist then left him to his own devices for some hours, but when he returned the pupil was only able to show him a very meagre result, some three or four sentences. Again the task was given, and this time the master stayed away a much longer time. Annoyed by the imposition of what he regarded as a silly exercise, the student sat down determined to write *all* about the fish. The state of annoyance served to put him on his mettle, and he was still writing busily when his teacher returned after some hours.

I want you to tackle your meditation in somewhat the same way; not with annoyance, but with a determination and pertinacity equal to that shown by the naturalist's pupil. You will find that, once you have mastered the techniques involved in meditation, you will not complain, as a rule, of lack of ideas.

You may be surprised by the nature of the meditation subjects which are given you. To many people meditation is a quiet reverie on emotionally tinged "spiritual" subjects. Such ideas are, of course, used, but it is necessary for us to have a well-balanced mental diet. For this reason the subjects are carefully chosen. During our correspondence you have revealed the general make-up of your character, and made known to me your natural line of approach. It is for this reason that the meditation subjects which you will receive may puzzle you, for you will find them to be the exact opposites of those which you would have chosen for yourself. It would be easy for you to meditate along the line of your natural inclination and neglect that which did not appeal to you. In this case, however, such progress as you might make would be very lop-sided, and I do not propose to train you in unbalance.

You will therefore learn to meditate on ideas which do not possess the interest which would make them attractive to you, and I expect you will not care for the effort involved. Believe me, however, it is absolutely essential that you receive a balanced training, and I should not be doing my duty if I permitted you to escape this necessary mental discipline.

You will find that these basic exercises in meditation are of two kinds. One in which you are asked to build up certain mental pictures is known as "image formation", and the other, in which images already in the mind are allowed to rise into consciousness, is known as "image recollection".

The first class of exercise is a very important method of training the visualizing power. Here we are using the term "visualizing" in a somewhat different way. We usually think of visualization in its literal sense, as the building up of pictures derived from the sense of sight, but occult visualization is the building of a composite mental image made up of impressions which have been received through all the five senses. Let me give you an example. You may be asked to build up the mental picture of a waterfall, say, the Niagara Falls. In this case you will have to make, not merely a picture of what the Falls look like, but also what they sound like, what the waters taste like, the scents which arise, and the feel of the rushing waters on the body.

The very fact of having to build this composite image in its fullness helps in the meditation, since the mind desires change, and, if jammed on just one point in the mental picture, will pass into a condition of auto-hypnosis. Useful though such a state can be, as you will discover at a later stage, it is not a desirable condition when one is beginning training in meditation. There is a very interesting simile used by Professor Ernest Woods in his book on concentration. He likens the mind to a fish swimming in a lake. In the centre of the lake is an island, and the fish is required to observe the general scenery on it. There are two ways in which he can do this. One is by sticking his nose in the muddy island bank, and trying to keep his attention fixed on what he sees. The other, and far more effective way, is for him to swim slowly round the island, and record all he sees in his circular journey. It is this second method which you have to follow in this initial training.

By varying the mental point of view by altering the emphasis on one set of pictures in favour of another, you should succeed in building a clear and comprehensive picture. This picture will be in three dimensions, will be "in the round", not merely a flat image. As you will see at a later date, when you are building the mental forms which are used as the channels of elemental energy of various grades, this visualization in the round enables you to build up really effective thought-forms.

Let us now consider the second type of meditation, "allowing the images to rise". Here the conscious mind is confined to clearing a space in which the latent images of the depths are allowed to rise to the surface. I am reminded here of the technique of certain Oriental magicians who train their seers first to see, in the magic mirror or ink-pool, the appearance of a man sweeping the area of vision therein. Then into this cleared space the visions are evoked. You will find that this "Preparation of the Place of Working" is a very important part of practical magical ceremonial, but just at present we are considering it only in what may be termed its minor manifestations.

There are certain technical devices by means of which this clearing of the mind can be done, and the one which I am about to describe is the one which I think is perhaps the best.

You have begun the work of building up definite thought-images, and this next part of your meditation discipline will develop your power in this respect. Here the "Composition of the Place" is begun by building up around you a mental picture of a wall of light separating you from the outer world. This circular wall of light you should visualize as silver in colour, and see it moving around you in a clockwise direction. It will help you to do this if you draw the line of this protecting barrier around you with your right hand in the air, at the same time turning slowly from left to right as you do so, and keeping clearly in your mind the "intention" to shut out all external conditions for the period of the exercise. The mental screen is now protected from the greater part of the drifting thought atmosphere in which we are immersed all our lives, and you are ready to observe the images which your own mind can produce.

As you sit with the mind thus withdrawn from outer things, you will find that certain mental images keep rising in consciousness. At first these may be very mixed and chaotic, but with practice you will find that certain groups of thoughts keep on coming up into the mental field. Whatever they may be, whether they are pleasant or otherwise, do not allow them to move you emotionally. Merely observe them as they arise, and then quietly, without any strained effort, visualize yourself as pushing them through the protecting wall and out of the mental field. They will possibly come up again and again, but as you calmly, and without emotional strain, dispose of them in this way, they will eventually lose their power to rise, and will no longer trouble you.

This preliminary work is not quite so easy as it sounds, but when once you have established it as an automatic habit, you will have acquired a most valuable power.

It is of no use, however, to clear the mental field unless we are going to do some work in it, so the next part of the exercise is to build up pictures of a particular type. We have two kinds of work to do: the building-up of images, and the recalling of images already made. It is best, therefore, to start our work by deliberately building up images, and so to train the visualizing faculty.

In my next letter I will give you the basic instructions on posture and breathing. You may think that the way in which I am teaching you is somewhat disjointed—in this instance I have broken off the instructions for the mental exercises, and returned to quite another subject. Do not let this worry you; there is a very definite reason for it. Again and again you will find me breaking the sequence of orderly instruction in this way, and at a later date you will more fully appreciate my reasons for doing so.

## SPECIMEN PAGE OF A MAGICAL DIARY.

### GRADE: E. A.

**Morning Salute**    Given at correct time.

**Noon Salute.**    Missed. Forgot.

**Evening Salute.**    Given, but later than usual. (Visitors arrived suddenly.)

**Exercise in Meditation**    Was able to visualize the street well, but I noticed that I could only visualize part of it at a time—as though I was using a mental flash-light. Only those things in the beam were clear—the rest was blurred and indistinct.

**Special Notes.**    I find considerable difficulty in *starting* the meditation, despite my "clearing" efforts.

# CHAPTER IV

# POSTURE AND BREATHING

AS I promised, I am sending you the instructions as to posture and breathing. You assure me that you have studied the previous instructions very carefully, and feel that you are ready to start definite meditation. This is good, but you will realize, of course, that these first exercises are very elementary, so far as subject matter is concerned. At the same time they are very essential, since they will give you proficiency in this art of meditation. Think of them as dull but necessary tasks which fall to the lot of the apprentice. I well remember how very dull and tedious was the work I had to do when I first began my apprenticeship as an engineer. But I began to see later on how it had helped me to become proficient. In this sphere of magical work the principle is implicit: "Learn by doing" is the motto for the apprentice.

Now let us deal with the postures, or, as they are called in the east, the *asanas*. It is obvious that the way in which we sit determines to some extent the blood flow in the body. It also affects the flow of the fine etheric currents which circulate through the "etheric double" of the body. For the control of these finer force-currents many forms of exercise have been elaborated, but for the purposes of your training we shall only deal with those which are the basic groundwork. As I have told you before, it is just because they *are* basic that they are of the utmost importance. Should you neglect them, your later work will be faulty. A young friend of mine was "evacuated" to the country during the last war. He was unfortunately unable to carry on his education in a normal manner and with customary regularity. At a later date, when he began to study for his profession, he found that the gaps in his early education were such hindrances to further work, that he was compelled to start again and fill them in systematically. In the same way the mind, being habit-forming will establish bad habits of meditation if it is not trained in the right ones. These bad habits are most difficult to correct. To take an example: any self-taught typist who has become used to bad habits of typing—the hunt-and-peck methods—and has had to break away from them will find it far more difficult to master the new and correct ones than it would have been if she had started with them in the first place.

The old habit has first to be broken down before the new one can be established. You may think I am labouring this point, but my reasons are simple. I do not wish you to waste your time and energy, and equally, I do not wish to waste my own by having to assist you in the overcoming of wrong habits of meditation.

The most commonly used posture in the east is the one which I have referred to as the *padmasana* or "Lotus" position. As I have told you it is a difficult one for most Europeans. At the same time it is a very efficient method of re-directing certain etheric currents in the "double", and at a later stage I will give you a modification of it. In our western schools we usually employ what is known as the "god-form" posture. It is achieved in this manner: sit straight upright in your chair with the spine as erect as possible; avoid being too "poker-backed". Remember that the spine has a slight natural curve of its own. Therefore sit straight up but be careful not to strain the back. The feet should be placed squarely on the floor, the knees kept close together and the hands should be resting on the knees. Do not cross the feet or clasp the hands together in this exercise. The posture is that of some of the Egyptian statues of Pharaohs. As I have told you, the best seat is a fairly hard chair, and if you *must* have a cushion, then it should be a fairly firm one. If such a cushion makes it difficult for you to place your feet firmly on the floor, then I am afraid you must either discard the cushion, find a lower chair, or obtain a foot-rest.

Now you must begin to relax. There is much misunderstanding about this idea of relaxation, and, as it is fundamental to all occult work, I want to deal with it as fully as I can. First you cannot relax correctly until you have discovered for yourself what tensions you habitually maintain. For this reason, therefore, the first part of relaxation is the deliberate attempt to locate the various points of tension in your body. Then you will have to practise both the induction of tension in any part at will and also the exact opposite—the reduction of tension in any part at will. You will be doing the equivalent of the experiments in gear changing which must be made by the "learner-driver". In the mental field your work will be of equal importance.

Start then, with the top of the head. As you sit in your "god-form" position, direct your attention to the top of your head and observe what tensions you are maintaining there. You will probably be as surprised as I was to find that you habitually tense your scalp muscles. Owing to the fact that normally, we do not employ these muscles consciously, we are liable to forget that they can be tensed, and so a habit of involuntary tension is built up. For the time being, merely observe whether this tension does, or does not, exist. Then shift your attention to the forehead and the face generally. You will most certainly find many tensions here. Then pass down to the throat, the chest, the abdomen, and finally to the ankles and feet. Now record carefully, on the first page of your diary, the various tension points you have found, and so conclude the first part of this examination. Now you must consider with care why these tensions are being maintained. It may be that owing to defective vision or unsuitable glasses, you are straining the muscles of the eyes and face, or perhaps you are undergoing some kind of mental strain? Whatever the cause, the muscular tensions must be eliminated. The purely physical causes such as unsuitable glasses, can be fairly easily dealt with but the mental causes are more difficult. However the important thing is to realize that they exist and then half the battle is won.

The regular practice of relaxation will usually put things straight. Having noted all the tensions of the body you are now ready for the next stage of the exercise. The foregoing tensions are involuntary, so the next step is to initiate voluntary tensions. That is to say, go over your body in the same way as before, but this time you will deliberately tense the muscles, observing, at the same time, the sensations which arise. When you have done this, sweep your attention again over the body, but this time deliberately relax each set of muscles. This is more difficult, since after you have gone on to a new area, you will find that you have involuntarily tensed up some of the preceding muscles, and you will have to start again. As a matter of fact, it is much the best thing to practise with only a part of the body in the early stages of training, and to become proficient in relaxing that part. Having achieved this, your relaxation may be extended to the next area until you have gone over the whole body.

Now we come to the most difficult part of this exercise. You have learnt to relax, and you have also practised deliberate tensioning of the muscles. The next stage is to arrive at a balance point between these two. Having arrived at a point of real relaxation, you must not allow yourself to drift into a lazy, hazy mental state, but must preserve a poised condition in which, although relaxation is good you are ready for immediate action should occasion demand. You will find that this poised condition is most difficult to attain, and only after repeated efforts will the mental "trick" be gained. Just as in learning to ride a cycle, the trick of balance is quite suddenly acquired, so it is with this particular subconscious mental habit. Once you have gained it, however, it will become automatic.

So we have three stages in this part of the exercise. First, the location of tensions. Then the relaxing of tensions, and finally the establishing of a poised muscular condition. The first part will not need to be repeated once you have located, and dealt with, the causes of these involuntary tensions, but the other two are essential parts of the exercise and must always be carried out.

After steady practice, you will be able to obtain complete relaxation and correct poise, and some part of this must have been acquired before you proceed to the next part of the work. As I warned you, this preliminary work can become monotonous, but it is vital.

Now we come to the matter of breathing exercises. At a later point in your training you will be taught certain special breathing exercises, but the one I am giving you now will be quite sufficient for you for the time being. It has been observed that there is a very real connection between the rate of breathing and the emotional activity of the mind. You must have noticed, of course, that when you are in a highly emotional state of consciousness your breathing rate is considerably increased. If, on the other hand, your emotions are not aroused, your breathing tends to become much slower. This correlation between the emotional states and the act of breathing was noted long ago and advantage was taken of it, the reason being that it is a reversible thing. Slow down the emotional surges of the mind, and the breathing slows down too; the reverse is equally true, slow down the breathing and the emotions calm at once. Upon this simple fact the basic breathing exercise has been constructed. It will be helpful if you try it out for yourself, and find out how this linking action works. Breathe rapidly and observe the results which you obtain. Quite apart from the emotional effects, you will find there are certain bodily reactions, which are due to the excessive oxygen intake. Incidentally, if you are engaged all day in a sedentary occupation, this rapid breathing helps to oxygenate the blood stream, and is beneficial in a purely physical sense. But if you use such a rapid breathing exercise, do not overdo it. It forms no part of the exercise itself.

Having observed the effects of such rapid breathing, try slowing down the breathing rate. Again you will find that there are certain physical effects, and again there is a point at which you must stop, for the present at least. As you have read in my former book, there is a real danger in misunderstanding or misapplying some of the instruction. Particularly is this the case when you are told to "hold the breath". As I pointed out, there is a tendency to inflate the lungs and then to close the mouth and hold the breath in by muscular tension. This can place a severe strain on the lungs, and however necessary it may be under certain physical conditions it must not be used in the breathing exercises.

We will now consider the first breathing exercise. Having assumed the meditation posture which has already been described, and having relaxed, breathe in through the nose and fill the lungs as far as you can. I say, as far as you can, for as a rule we are seldom using the full capacity of the lung system. What is known as "shallow" breathing is the general method of breathing, and it is possibly responsible for much of the ill-health we see around us. More particularly is this the case where people are pursuing sedentary occupations. From the purely physical viewpoint, therefore, these breathing exercises are of value. From the magical standpoint they are still more valuable, as I shall again point out at a later stage.

In the beginning of your training, however, you should aim at gradually increasing the volume of air you can draw in without strain. Remember, the lungs must be allowed to stretch in order to take in this extra supply, and if you have been using only shallow breathing all your life, it is somewhat difficult for the lungs suddenly to accommodate the new rhythm. I am stressing this point because, although it seems very simple, it is most important.

Now you have inhaled what is, for the present at least, a full charge of air. Use a rhythm in this. Count mentally, one, two, three, four, for your inbreathing, and then try to base your speed upon some natural rhythm around you, or upon the ease with which your lungs work. Perhaps at the beginning, you will find it a considerable effort to take these deep breaths, and this will impose a natural check upon your speed. However, if you count mentally and acquire the habit of correctly timing your counting, you will find that there is a definite duration of time which you will establish for this inbreathing.

It is now necessary to hold the breath, and if you have used this count of four, then the breath should be held for as long as it takes you to count two in the same rhythm. Hold the breath by keeping the ribs in the position they are in at the end of the inspiration, and keep the throat relaxed. It should now be possible for you, by tapping sharply on your chest, to expel the air, or some of it, simply by this action. When you have gained proficiency in this you have taken the first step towards real breath control. Now you must exhale. Again use the fourfold count: one, two, three, four, as you release the chest muscles. You must now use these muscles to squeeze out, as it were, the remaining air. As a general rule we only use a small part of the lungs, and when we exhale, there are considerable areas of lung which are not used in their entirety. In these areas, carbon dioxide gas, which should normally be exhaled, is liable to accumulate, and this prevents full use of the lung machinery. So squeeze out, without strain, as much of the used air as possible, and again hold the lungs, this time in an empty state, while you count, one, two. Then begin again as you have been taught.

Do not overdo the number of deep controlled breaths at this stage of your training. At a later date, when you will be using more advanced forms of breathing, you will be able to increase them, but for the present restrict yourself to six complete inhalations and exhalations. When I want you to go further in this I will let you know.

This breathing exercise is the only one which you will be given which is merely a breathing exercise. At a later stage you will receive more elaborate exercises involving the breath; but they are based upon a different principle. I think it may be helpful if I briefly outline it here.

I have referred to the "etheric double" or "vital body" as it is also termed, and it is with this double that further exercises will deal. In the vital body, as the name implies, the life forces circulate in their appropriate channels. But the vital body is not built of ordinary physical matter as is the grosser vehicle we use during our earthly life. The vital body is composed of a finer type of substance, and is the dividing line between dense matter and the subtle matter of the Inner Planes. It is, in fact, sometimes known as the "linking-body", since it forms a link between the physical and the more subtle types of matter. Upon it, as upon a mould, the physical body is built and all the processes of life in the material body depend upon the vital forces which are channelled by it. In the vital body are the connecting points which link the two levels of the physical and the so-called "astral". It will therefore be clear that the vital body carries not only the life-currents of the physical body, but also that it forms the bridge between the physical brain-consciousness and the types of consciousness of the inner planes. It is well to remember that this normal waking consciousness is only part of our full consciousness. In psychological work we speak of the subconscious, conscious, and super-conscious levels of the mind, and of these three, the physical brain consciousness is very much the junior partner. At the same time, although in many ways it is inferior to the other two, it is the growing point of our mental evolution, and as such it is of the very greatest importance.

I do want to emphasize this point, for so many of the books you will read which deal with these subjects, give the impression that the physical body and the physical plane consciousness are in some way evil, and must be abandoned for what is referred to as the "higher" consciousness. This is a very old teaching. It is found in the Neo-Platonic philosophy, and in the form of the Manichean heresy it found its way into the teachings of the early Christian Church. Although repudiated by the Church it has reappeared throughout the centuries. One of its forms is what is known as "Puritanism", and when the eastern teachings were first introduced to the west the old error found new ground.

In this school, of which you are now an apprentice member, we entirely repudiate it. The Qabalistic philosophy, which is at the core of all our teaching, views the physical world and the physical body in quite a different way. So far from regarding matter as evil, it is thought of as the "luminous garment of the Eternal", and as being in itself the manifestation of the Eternal Being. There is then, from this viewpoint, no *intrinsic* evil in matter, and the physical plane is just as "spiritual" as any of the so-called "higher planes". But it is quite definitely a limiting plane. It compels consciousness to concentrate itself within certain fairly narrow limits, and to those who have had any contact with the abounding life of the inner planes, it does seem definitely inferior to them. Since, however, our personal consciousness is the growing point of our mental evolution, it is essential for us to be able to use the physical consciousness efficiently. It is of very little use to develop the "higher consciousness" if it is not possible, at the same time, to correlate it with the waking brain-consciousness. The descent of the god-like consciousness into the physical can only result, in such a case, in a blinding inrush of light which, so far from being "illumination" will blind the normal awareness, just as a sudden beam of intense light will temporarily blind the physical eyes. So what we aim at in the training of students is the gradual development of the normal consciousness until it is capable of being taken up into the inner forms of awareness.

So in all your training bear this cardinal teaching in mind: "That which God hath cleansed, that call not thou common." Never despise or denigrate either the physical plane or the body which is built of the substance of that plane. I shall constantly remind you of these things in the course of our work together, and I do want you to write this fundamental law upon your mental tablets, so that in all your magical work it remains as a conditioning factor therein.

I want here to give you a very serious warning about the use of the psycho-physical exercises. one based upon my own experience. It is very necessary, of course, to take into account the physical body and its etheric counterpart, and there exists in the east a considerable amount of teaching and practice which is concerned with this aspect of training. This is commonly termed "Hatha Yoga", and many people who are working, or attempting to work, along Eastern lines are wont to give us portentous warnings of the dangers of Hatha Yoga. There is truth in what they say, but the abuse of a thing should not prevent us making a wise use of it. In our school there are the same teachings and practices as those of the Hatha Yogis, but they are adapted to the physical and psychic make-up of western pupils.

However, we are all somewhat apt to make mistakes, especially in the period of our training when we begin to think that, as, so far, we have satisfactorily done the work set us, we can add something from another source, a book we have read, or the teachings we have heard from other organizations. I was no exception to this, and although I was warned against mixing the exercises, I thought I knew best, so I tacked on to my routine meditation work one of the yoga breathing exercises. It certainly produced results, but these were of two kinds. I developed an increased psychic awareness, but at the same time I most thoroughly disorganized part of my psychological machinery. It took me a long time, even with the help of my own teacher, before I was able to clear the effects of my ill-advised action. I am anxious that you should not fall into the same trap; it is far too costly a method of acquiring experience.

# CHAPTER V

# MEDITATION

THE first mental exercises you have been given are, as you will remember, the "Preparation of the Place" and the "Calling back". Of these, the latter seems more appropriate for meditation during the evening, rather than in the early morning. It is not advisable, however, to meditate *late* in the the evening when the body is tired and the fine etheric double is strained. Any meditation done late at night should be of a quiet non-strenuous nature. I will tell you more about this later.

So you will start with the calling-back exercise, and then proceed to the preparation of the place. When you have done this, you can approach the definite subject which has been set for you. I expect you will be rather disappointed when you find what it is, therefore, before I describe it, I will give you some idea of the principle involved. You are familiar, of course, with the statement that all knowledge is ultimately based on the impressions received through the senses. By many physiologists this is limited to impressions derived through the physical senses alone, but we have found by experience that there are very many impressions which come into the mind through the *nonphysical* senses. In this first series of exercises, however, we shall be dealing with the knowledge gained through the material senses.

I have told you of two types of exercises: one in which images are allowed to rise in the mental field, and the other where the mental images are deliberately formed. It is therefore necessary that the student should cultivate the power of observation which results in the building up of a stock of clearly cut mental images which can be recalled at will into the consciousness. People vary tremendously in this respect. Some possess what is termed an "eidetic" memory and are able to recall at will very clear-cut images, while others can only summon up vague and misty forms, though these are usually charged with a considerable amount of emotional feeling. But vague drifting ideas are not what is desired. It is very necessary, therefore, that you begin to form definite pictures in your mind. Incidentally, this term "pictures" includes not only the *visual* images, but the olfactory, tactile, gustatory, and sound impressions as well. Proficiency in this all-round image building is gained only by the development of a greatly neglected faculty, that of *observation*.

It is therefore very necessary for you to cultivate this power. This may best be done by using the events of the day as your field of work. For instance, you are on your way to work and are travelling in a bus or train. There will be many others around you, all intent on their own affairs. There will be a strong temptation to withdraw into yourself, to vaguely "day-dream" or perhaps immerse yourself in the contents of the morning paper. Instead, having begun your magical training, you will avail yourself of this opportunity to develop your powers of observation. I am not asking you to emulate the feats of Sherlock Holmes, as recorded by the late Sir Arthur Conan Doyle, but I am suggesting that you turn your attention outwards to what is going on around you, and observe deliberately, without impertinent staring, what those around you are doing, and what is happening in the streets through which you are passing. This sounds very dull and humdrum, but it is really a very important part of your training.

Apart from anything else, you will remember that one of the objects of life on this physical world is to develop the power of control over matter, or so we believe. This covers far more than the mere conquest of physical happenings, for the moral and ethical aspects of life must also be brought into line with the eternal spiritual principles which lie behind all manifestation. But first things first, and so we must first begin to conquer in the purely material levels. All subjective emotional "spirituality" which endeavours to escape from the moil and toil of everyday life on the physical plane is an "escapism", and although we may occasionally allow ourselves the luxury of a rest "behind the lines", we must always remember that we have to return to the battle. This battle of life is one in which we must all take our part, and to endeavour to escape from it entirely is "cowardice in the face of the enemy"; it is also of no real avail, since, at one point or other in the future, we *must* face up to those disagreeable things which we have tried to avoid.

I know this sounds rather hard and somewhat removed from the soothing teachings which are so often put forward as spiritual and mystical instruction, and I daresay you may be thinking as you read this, of those men and women who are members of the contemplative Orders of the Christian Church, as well as those in other religions who follow a similar path. I can only say that on the path of High Magic spiritual soothing syrup is not dispensed, any more than it is on the Mystic Way. Spiritual consolation is available, one is not left indefinitely in the Slough of Despond or the Giant's Castle. There are ministrations which are given us, and there are, increasingly, periods of refreshment. But "*after* labour, refreshment". There is a rhythm in these things. As for the contemplatives, if you were to have the vocation for their path, you would find that it is not mere escapism, nor retreat from life, but a most strenuous endeavour to share in the life of the world *after another fashion*. But, to every man his own master, and as far as you are concerned, your vocation is to the Magical Path, and you come, therefore, under its particular training and discipline. So it is that instead of advising our apprentices to meditate on lofty things, we start them off on very mundane exercises. To use a phrase which is often misused by occult students, we start from below and work upwards. At the same time, of course, you are instructed to look upwards and to strive without ceasing to lift up your consciousness to higher levels.

I have used the word "higher", but, as I have told you, there is no such thing as an absolute differentiation between higher and lower. These terms are relative, and so many occult students have made the great mistake of despising what they termed the "lower planes" in their desire to reach the "higher planes". This, according to our teaching, is a fundamental error, and we are instructed to give our apprentices an entirely different point of view. As you are aware, our school is based on the Qabalistic philosophy which is the Hebrew esoteric tradition, and one of its basic teachings is that not only did the Eternal Being whom we call God "create" this universe, but also that He is present throughout all its manifestations, and all grades of matter are, in fact, actual expressions of His essential nature. So the physical plane is just as "spiritual" as any of the finer grades of matter which are usually referred to as the "higher planes". In our tradition we refer to these as the "inner planes". This avoids the false idea that spirit and matter are eternally opposed to each other. This erroneous idea has plagued the esoteric schools throughout their history, and in the guise of what is termed the "Manichean heresy" it entered the Christian Church in its early days, and here it has shown its face from time to time throughout the centuries. The Catholic Church repudiated it, but the strain persisted, and after the Reformation, when the protestant churches broke away from Rome, it reappeared in some of the new religious organizations.

We, however, regard matter, of whatever grade it may be, as the "luminous garment of the Eternal", a living garment, part of the Eternal, or to be more precise, a direct expression of the infinite life. It follows therefore, that our material bodies and material nature around us are equally "holy", and neither of them should be despised. I have stressed this idea in order that you may start free from

the mental blinkers of the dichotomy of "high" and "low". Strive
always to realize that the Eternal is manifesting in all things, yes, all
things both in heaven and earth and in the waters under the earth,
and that in very truth, as St Paul said, quoting a Greek poet, "in
Him we live and move and have our being."

Having considered this important point, let us return to our meditation training. The habit of observation must be cultivated if you
would build up and use the mental images, and the best way is as I
have indicated. Care must be taken however, not to use this training
in observation as a means of "listening-in" to other people's private
conversation. I have known this to happen, and the apprentice concerned, when accused of it, blandly replied that he was training his
power of attending to sound! It may seem a small point, but it is a
very vital one that under *no circumstances* whatsoever, whether by
psychic or physical means, must we pry into the private lives of
others. This prohibition is based upon a certain principle which is to
be found in the Bible. There it is said, "Cursed is the man that re-
moveth his neighbour's landmark." In the purely material and agri-
cultural conditions of primitive life this was a very real danger, and
in more sophisticated ways it is still present to-day. In another great
Order, this prohibition is phrased thus: "Cursed is he who breaks a
superficies."

"What is this boundary, this landmark?" you may ask. To answer
that we must consider certain details of the structure of man. We are
far too prone to think of our mind as being in some way boxed up in
our skull, though just whereabouts therein we are uncertain. But the
truth is that the mind is in all parts of the body. It would be more
correct to say, not that the mind is in the body, but rather that the
body is in the mind. The mind field extends around the body, just as
the magnetic field extends around the actual steel magnet. This field
of force around each one of us is termed the "aura", and it is within
our own particular surround, our own aura, that we have to work.
Its limits form what is sometimes called the "Ring-Pass-Not". This
term is applied in the esoteric schools, also to signify the boundary of
the universe, for we teach that the whole universe is held in the consciousness of the Eternal, just as the little universe of ourselves is
held within the consciousness of that spirit which is our real Self.

So the Ring-Pass-Not must be respected, and we must never tres-
pass in another's field of working. As you will see, on reflection, this
fundamental law covers a very wide field, and it is important that you
should build it most thoroughly into your philosophy, for, as you
begin to bring into action some of the latent powers within you the

temptation will be strong to use them to "influence people", and to cause them to work for your advantage. There are very many books published at the present time which purport to teach you to influence others *in your own interest*. This practice is forbidden in the esoteric schools of both the east and west. Should you infringe this rule, you will soon find that you have ceased to be my apprentice. Always remember that the motive of your work is summed up in the words "I desire to know in order to serve." If it is necessary for you to use your powers for the good of any other person, then you will be given the opportunity, but any attempt to apply such powers without the consent of the person concerned is fraught with danger. At a later stage in your training you will again come up against this law, for it is a fundamental teaching, not an arbitrary rule.

Well now, you are about to begin your training in observation. Here are a few points to observe. Do not concentrate your attention on one particular person or thing; allow your observation to range over as wide a field as possible, and let that field include the peculiar activities of buses and car drivers, to say nothing of the vagaries of dogs and children. It is no part of your training to be so intent on one particular object that you are knocked down by a bus or car; nor to disorganize all the traffic by "jay walking" blithely across a busy street. In either case you might end up by becoming a resident of the inner planes before the time was ripe.

(I have known an instance of this in the case of a psychic who was in the habit of "opening-up" her psychic perception without any regard to what was happening around her on the physical plane).

Here is a good exercise in observation, an exercise which will develop that power of allowing the images to rise.

Ask yourself what you know of the scenery of the road in which you live; what types of houses are to be found in it; how many windows has the biggest house; what is the difference between the two sides of the street. Formulate these questions, and try to answer them. You will probably find, as I did when I first started doing this exercise, that although you may have gone down that street some hundreds of times, you cannot with any certainty give a detailed description of it. It is therefore good practice to give it a closer scrutiny as you pass down it, then you will be able at a later stage to use both the images you have "built" up and those you can summon by the developed power of observation. Do not try to do this in one fell swoop, as it were, or you will end by observing too much at once; before you have trained your mind to record the sense-images in an orderly fashion. I have spoken of visual imagery alone, but it is obvious that you should observe also the impressions received from the other senses.

A variant of this exercise is the so-called "Kim's game". As you will remember Kim undergoes a test for this very power of observation. He is shown a tray of jewels, and after a minute's steady observation of them the tray is covered and he has to say what is on it. Actually this is a rather difficult exercise for the beginner, though it does give some idea of the extent of his powers of observation. I would suggest to you that you occasionally use Kim's game as a check on your progress in observation.

As with all these exercises, there is a definite principle involved, and it is left to your own ingenuity to devise other exercises based upon this basic idea. In this way you begin to work intelligently, and you are not so likely to be too dependent on me. In all these things always strive to find the underlying principle involved, never simply follow the letter of the instructions. This is a most important point. It is true that you may not always be able to grasp all the significance of any particular exercise, but you should be able to get a general idea of the point behind it. If you cannot do this then in all probability the fault lies in myself. So whenever, after careful study of any exercise, you cannot grasp the principle involved please tell me, and I will do my best to make it clearer. Never think that to query instructions in this way will show you to be backward in your work. We are all rather chary of displaying our ignorance, more particularly when we are under training; but, as I have already told you, the basic foundations must be laid without any gaps due to inability to learn certain essentials. There is another point involved here. The mind being a creature of habit and inclined to laziness, will sometimes try to dodge the performance of some exercise by a curious blurring of perception. It would almost appear that there is a sort of mental blind which descends when an effort is made to get at the root idea of any particular teaching, and it is necessary, when this occurs, to repeat your efforts. If you persevere in this, the mind gives in, and the mental "block" disappears. It will probably recur over and over again, but if you persevere it will finally die away, and the new habit will have been established. I cannot stress too strongly the importance of this endeavour to escape from the tyranny of following the letter of the law without any understanding of the principles upon which the instruction is based. Of course, there may be exercises given whose *full* significance cannot be grasped until further teaching gives you the relevant clue, but it should always be possible for you to get a good general comprehension of the basic ideas concerned. If this should not happen to be the case, then, as I have said, the fault must lie with me.

You will often find when you receive my instructions, that it will help you to absorb them if you first of all read them through very carefully and then leave them to "incubate" for a time. You can then return to them and you will find them to be more easily understood. This is because your subconscious mind has been doing some preliminary spade-work on them. This particular activity of the subconscious should be used to the full, it saves a lot of conscious mental struggle.

Here I want to give you some instruction with visual pictures. There are two ways of visualizing any particular object or diagram. One is by a wholesale effort in which the entire picture or diagram is visualized. The drawback to this method is that should one line or detail be forgotten, the whole picture is falsified. This is particularly the case when visualizing a diagram such as that very important *mandala*, the "Tree of Life". The other method of visualizing is first to get an idea of the underlying principle of whatever picture you are using. By establishing the idea in your mind, you will be able to clothe it with the correct images. Give your picture a name, and use this name to evoke from your memory the correct images, but be precise in your naming. Thus "men at work" is too vague, but "men digging up roadway" will enable the correct memory images to arise, and will facilitate their full emergence. In the next instructions, I shall begin to give you the general idea of the great glyph, "The Tree of Life", and you will then be asked to attempt to draw it and let me have the results.

I remember another pupil of mine who resented this routine work. He considered that as he knew all about it, there was no need for repeated drawings of the diagram. But it is a very necessary discipline, more particularly if the student's drawing technique is weak. At a later date you will be asked to draw this glyph from memory, and if you have not trained yourself to understand the underlying principles on the Tree, your drawing will show this lack of comprehension. So do not be annoyed if you have to make these drawings, and if I severely criticize them.

When you begin to work with the Tree, you will find that all this preliminary work in observation will stand you in good stead, for the work you will have to do with that great glyph falls into the two divisions we have already noted: the building of images and the recalling of them at will.

Do not forget to record your results in your magical diary. I know, from practical experience, how mortifying it is to have to send in the diary with about half the entries marked "Forgot to do meditation", or "Forgot to give Salutes", or "Just could not meditate to-day"! Until the mind has been trained entries such as these are bound to recur with monotonous persistence in the diary! But they must be recorded, even though you feel ashamed of them.

Often I wished the earth would swallow me up when I received back my diary, with the addition of scribbled comments, of a more or less sarcastic nature, against the entries. But just as an apprentice in any trade must be prepared to undergo the criticism of the craftsman under whom he is training, so also must you. There is, of course, constructive as well as destructive criticism; as a general rule I shall criticize your efforts from the constructive angle. There may, however, be occasions, as there were in my own training, when only a definitely destructive criticism can be given. When this is the case, I hope that neither of us will be found wanting: I to make it and you to take it!

# CHAPTER VI

# THE TREE OF LIFE

YOU will have observed, when you read my book *The Magician*, that we of the Western Tradition use as our *mandala*, or meditation Glyph, a most wonderful composite symbol which comes to us from the esoteric school of the Hebrews.

It is called *Otz Chiim* or "The Tree of Life", and is defined among us as "the mighty, all-embracing glyph of the universe and the soul of man". I do not propose to describe it in detail, since a far better exposition of it has already been given to the public by one of the greatest of our western teachers, the late Dion Fortune, in a book entitled *The Mystical Qabalah*. This book will give you the best outline of the Tree of Life, and it is imperative that you obtain and use it, both as a textbook and a source of reference.

If you cannot obtain it through the publisher, I advise searching in the second-hand shops or writing to one of the many second-hand booksellers who advertise in the various occult and psychic publications. It may seem that you are being set a somewhat difficult task, but this is in line with the general practice of the magical schools. As Eliphas Levi, who wrote extensively on these subjects, has pointed out, the man who rises at dawn and goes out to cut the branch which he then proceeds to form into his magical wand, will develop his will in so doing, and this principle is implicit in all magical training. Even as the apprentice in a trade is left to struggle to some extent with his new work, so also is the magical apprentice. Therefore put energy into the task of obtaining this book. When you have it, remember that it is not a book which can be read through at one sitting, nor is it in any way "light" reading. Far more teaching is to be found in it than appears from the first, or even twenty-first, reading. After many years of work in this field, I still find new avenues of thought opening up as I re-read it.

However, before you start to study the lore of the Tree as given in Dion Fortune's work, I want to give you a simple idea of what it is all about. Remember that behind the Tree is a great body of philosophic and theosophic doctrine which is known as the *Qabalah*.

The name signifies "from mouth to ear", i.e., it was a teaching which was transmitted orally from teacher to pupil. It was only in about the twelfth century that any of it was written down, and even then it was not very clearly defined. The Western Tradition is like a river which receives the tributaries from many sources, and is enriched thereby. In this it resembles the Christian Church, and the same simile was applied to that church by St Augustine.

However, though the Tradition has received waters from many strange fountains, the core of its teaching is organized around this mighty glyph of the Tree of Life, whose leaves are for the healing of the nations, microcosmically and macrocosmically.

The Tree is in reality a very wonderful card-index system, and I want you, in the first place, to use it as such. Later on you will find we have many other uses for it, but in your first exercises it must be used in its most elementary form. It is to be built into your mental content in such a way that it becomes what is sometimes referred to as a "reference-frame". All the multiplicity of detail which is to be found in life can be found a place on the Tree, and as the definition I have given you indicates, the circumstances of your own inner life, as well as those of the outer world, can be dealt with by the use of this symbol. You will learn, in this training, to "place on the Tree" all the factors which you will be asked to observe in life. It is a process of sorting out and classifying all the happenings of life in order to arrive at a definite pattern.

The subconscious mind is a great pattern former, but its own private mythology often bears very little relationship to the actual facts of life. It is therefore necessary to give it some foundation upon which it can build, in the same way that we give the bees in a beehive sheets of "foundation" wax, upon which they can build the honeycomb in an organized way. Left to themselves they do not work so neatly. Thus it is with your mind. If we want to build it up on the best lines, then we must have some pattern upon which to work.

You will see, as you study the Tree diagram, that there are ten circles joined together by twenty-two lines in a certain pattern, and the circles and lines together form the thirty-two Paths of the Ageless Wisdom. The circles or *Sephiroth**, as they are termed, represent the powers and forces of the universe, and also the points where your own individual consciousness comes into contact with those forces. The lines between them, usually known as the "Paths", represent the subjective inner world of consciousness which is common to both yourself and the planet on which you live. This idea of the earth as a living thing may amaze you, for we are so accustomed to thinking of it as a dead mineral ball whirling around the sun, that any idea of planetary spirits has been relegated to the superstitious past of the

*The ten circles are known in the plural as *Sephiroth*; the singular is *Sephirah*.

race. But esoteric science teaches that nothing in the whole universe is "dead", everywhere there is life, from the smallest atom to the greatest star. Neither does life cease to be anywhere; it fills the voids between the atoms. Indeed, according to our teaching, all manifestation is nothing more than the activity of the One Life. Herein we differ in some part from those who think of "creation" as the making of something which is apart from that which caused it to be. We think of created things as being the actual manifestations, under the veils of time and space, of the life of the Eternal.

If we should use a prayer, derived from the east, in which we implore God to lead us "from the unreal to the Real", we do not think that the life of the universe is less present in one plane than in another; *it is only our perception* with its limited range which prevents us from seeing that all is indeed a "theophany", a manifestation of the Pleroma, the Fullness of the Eternal. It is one of the aims of esoteric training to bring us to the point where we know this by experience, and have thereby developed or unfolded from within us that type of consciousness which is known as "cosmic consciousness". Remember, however, that other schools are also endeavouring to develop this form of consciousness in their pupils; avoid, therefore, attempting to pass superior judgement on them. Your task is to get on with the business of applying these teachings to yourself.

Now, I want you first of all, to get or make up a card-index system, with ten heading cards. Each of these cards is to be given the title of one of the *Sephiroth* on the Tree, and under the title the general idea of the significance of this particular station is to be written. Then, and this is most important, the rest of the card is to be filled in with a coloured circle; the symbolic representation of the sephira concerned. When you have made up your ten heading cards in this way, you are ready to begin your work with them, and you may do this as follows. Obtain other sub-cards, and then take your chosen *sephirah*, trying at the same time to discern in the world around you and in the circumstances of your own life, the working-out of the principle expressed by this *sephirah*.

Let me give you an example. We will take the *sephirah Geburah*; it is one of the stations on the Tree which lends itself to illustration. As you will see, if you consult the table, *Geburah* is usually termed "Fear", and its particular quality is held to be destruction. Now there are many occult students who attempt to by-pass this principle of destruction. They regard all destruction as evil. Indeed I have heard it put forth as an axiom that all that destroys is evil, and all that constructs is good. But this is an infantile view of life, and does not correspond to the facts. Here you must remember that the *sephiroth* on the side-pillars of the Tree are arranged in balancing pairs, and the opposite station to *Geburah* is *Gedulah* whose quality is constructive. You should here bear in mind that one of the magical statements is, "Equilibrium is the basis of the Great Work." This is beautifully expressed by Tennyson in the words which he puts into the mouth of the dying Arthur:

> The old order changeth, yielding place to new,
> And God fulfils Himself in many ways,
> Lest *one good custom* should corrupt the world.

Too great concentration of any one quality, or its persistence for too long a time *is* evil, for it is an unbalanced force: one of the "Kings of Edom", to use the *Qabalistic* term. When a power is working in this unbalanced way, we refer to it as being in the kingdom of the *Qlippoth*. Every station on the Tree, therefore has its obverse counterpart, and your work is to balance the forces in your own little microcosm, your own subjective world within. When you achieve this, in any degree whatsoever, then the corresponding forces in the universe will become responsive to your will.

Now let us study the action of our chosen *sephirah*. As we walk down the street, we see that demolition has started on some old and dilapidated houses which have been an eyesore for a long time. The workmen are busy with pick and shovel and bull-dozer, and soon there will be nothing there but a bare patch of ground. However we have been told by our local council that this plot is to be used for the building of a new school which will give to the neighbourhood a vastly improved education service. This is a good example of the activity of *Geburah*. But as we continue our walk down the street, we also see that an unoccupied house which was in quite good condition has been attacked by some irresponsible people, either children or adults, and the windows have been smashed, doors forced, and some of the woodwork stripped away. This is an example of purposeless destruction and comes under the heading of *Qlippothic* activity, unbalanced force, and is, therefore, evil. Not only can you see the activity of this *sephirah* and its unbalanced presentation in such obvious examples; it is also to be seen in all aspects of life. In your own body it is at work, for in the formative period of your growth, the building-up process goes on more actively than the breaking-down process, but gradually the breaking-down forces assume a greater power, and the body begins to break down. Now the balanced action of the complementary forces is "health", and as you will observe this condition of health is not confined to the purely physical plane. All the levels of your being must be balanced in this way if you would enjoy perfect health. The modern understanding of what the medical profession terms "psycho-somatic" treatment is based on the fact that all the levels of your being are affecting, and being affected by, each other.

Your task, therefore, in your work on the *sephirah* is to look out for its action in daily life, and to observe also what happens when its particular quality is either less or more manifest than is required for balance. You will have noticed that the question of "intention" comes into the picture, since it is the motive causing any particular action which determines whether it is "good" or "bad". There is also the larger picture of the community into which all such action is to be fitted. Here conflicting loyalties make decision difficult, and it is very necessary to exercise what has been called the first virtue on the Path, namely that of "Discrimination".

When, in your meditation work on the Tree, you are dealing with any one of the paired *sephiroth*, you will be required to observe the action of both, in order that you may appreciate this question of balance; but with those stations on the Tree which occupy what is known as the "Middle Pillar", a somewhat different method is used. It is still true that unbalance is possible on these *sephiroth*, just as with the others, but they have no complementary stations to balance them. They are in some measure, however, the balancing points between the paired *sephiroth*, and are the spheres wherein your consciousness works, as you will see from the Tree diagram.

There is a fourfold method of using the Tree of Life, and this is of the greatest importance in your training. The Tree, with all its stations and symbolism, can be, indeed it must be, considered from four different levels. Now here it is necessary for me to caution you against picturing these "levels", or "worlds" as they are termed in *Qabalistic* training, as being one above the other in space. Perhaps a radio analogy will help. Long waves, medium waves, and short waves can be received by us if we have a radio set which responds to them, but none of these three waves is above the other, and although we may speak of high waves or low waves, they all interpenetrate each other and are equally important. So it is with the Tree in the Four Worlds. Always remember this, because it is a cardinal point in our system of training.

This fourfold division is usually described under the following heads:

*Atziluth*. The world of Archetypes.
*Briah*. The world of Creation.
*Yetzirah*. The world of Formation.
*Assiah*. The world of Matter.

In practical meditation, this classification is used in this way. The particular quality of the *sephirah* which has been chosen as the subject for our attention is regarded from each one of these four aspects. Thus, if we take the *sephirah Geburah* again as our example, we shall study its action on each of these levels of manifestation. (You will remember that I told you that you would find that the monthly subject for your meditation exercise would give you more scope than at first seemed likely.)

In the *Qabalistic* system, we find that one of the root-ideas is that of "Adam Kadmon", the Heavenly Man, which is understood as the sum total of all manifesting forces in the universe. Pictured under this symbolic form, the various stations of the Tree are identified with definite areas of the body of the Heavenly Man. During the Middle Ages, this identification became somewhat naïve, but the basic ideas were retained. Curiously enough, when the great Swedish seer, Swedenborg, experienced the "illuminations" which enabled him to put out the great body of doctrine which forms the base of the Swedenborgian, or "New Church", he put forward this age-old concept of the Heavenly Man. But other systems of philosophy in the east have also had this same teaching, and in modern psychology we are finding that the symbol of the Heavenly Man is to be found in the depths of our mental being.

There is an occult maxim which is attributed to Hermes Trismegistus, though it is fairly evident that in its present form, it is of a much later period than the times of that somewhat shadowy figure. It declares, "As above, so below", and this doctrine of the correspondence which exists between the Macrocosm, the great universe, and the Microcosm, which is man, underlies all the occult philosophies of both east and west.

So, just as you must train yourself to see the operations of the various forces in the objective world around you, you must also study the action of those same energies in yourself, in your own subjective world.

In the outer world of manifestation, there are certain points which are taken as being the particular channels through which the living energies of the eternal are expressed, and in the *Qabalistic* philosophy these are equated with the sun and its planets. As you will see, as you continue your study of the Tree, there is implicit in it a very real astrological scheme; as, of course, there is in the eastern philosophical scheme. Astrology has fallen into disrepute, owing to the misuse of the teaching in both ancient and modern times, but in reality it is a lofty philosophy, *and as such has nothing whatever to do* with the "sun-sign" astrological prophecies given out by the national press!

But in our teaching, we refer not only to the stars outside ourselves, but to what are often called the "interior stars" which exist within us. This teaching, based upon the seership of generations of workers in this field, states that just as there are centres of the cosmic energy located in definite places in the outer universe, so there are similar centres of the same living power which are located in certain definite parts of our own inner universe. In the east these centres are commonly referred to as the *chakras* or "wheels", and to clairvoyant vision they do appear as small whirling vortices similar to fiery wheels. These *chakras* are described in many books, and are said to be seven in number. Different authorities give different centres as belonging to these seven, but in the main they agree on five or six of them. As I was taught in India, and have since verified for myself, there are many more such psychic centres, and although as a general rule the seven usually described will be active to some extent, it can and does happen that some peculiarity of temperament of training will cause another of these *chakras* to become active, while one of the usual seven will not be working so well.

In our system we give to these points of psychic activity the names of the planetary bodies, hence the term I have used: "interior stars". As you will see on your Tree diagram, these heavenly bodies are attributed to the *sephiroth*, and when you use the Tree as a subjective method, then you will find that the various planetary symbols are related to different areas of your body and to different psychic centres.

The *chakras* are the points where your subjective universe makes contact with the greater universe around you, and through them you not only receive sense impressions from the Inner Planes, but they also act as channels through which the energies of those levels make contact with you and arouse within you their own peculiar powers. Here is a very important point which I want to impress upon you. The powers and energies with which you work are cosmic forces which are ever working in all aspects of the created universe. These same forces are also at work in your own subjective universe, and the processes of esoteric training are designed to allow the microcosm to be the channel of the same cosmic energies, which will then well up within you. Do not be always looking outwards for these potencies. The outer energies are used to stimulate and induce the inner powers to manifest. As the title of one of the New Thought books puts it very aptly, "Within you is the Power".

Remember, however, that the principal *chakras* are very closely connected with what are known as the endocrine glands, those marvellous chemists of the body, and unwise concentration upon the psychic centres in the body can result in glandular unbalance. So beware of trying *unregulated* experiments, but stick to the meditations you are given. At a later date you will be encouraged to devise experiments, but by then you will have learnt to work with the underlying laws which govern them.

There is a very important principle which I want to explain to you at this stage of your training, and it is one which you must always keep in mind. It is, that the energies and forces with which you will be working, although welling up from within the depths of your own subjective self, *are not your own powers*, but aspects of the universal cosmic Life finding expression through you. To use a rough analogy; you press down an electric light switch and the electric current causes your lamp to light up. Now you did not make the electric current, neither is it your personal property, except so far as you have prepared a channel for it in your house and have paid for using it. In the same way the cosmic energies are at your personal disposal, but if you attempt to "make a corner" in them, or to draw upon them without due payment, or to misdirect them when you have got them, then you will find yourself in trouble.

You may ask, "what then, have I to pay for the use of these universal forces?" The answer is simple: you must offer sacrifice, and that sacrifice must be the offering-up of all the personal self to the service of God and man. Only thus can you hope to use the cosmic power with safety. Now many people, perhaps most people, equate "sacrifice" with "sorrow", and when they are asked to sacrifice, they feel that thereby they are losing something. But in all forms of training, and not in occult training alone, this principle of sacrifice is implicit. The trouble is that most of us, indeed the greater majority of us, regulate our lives on the "pleasure–pain" principle. This means that, like children, we attempt to hold on to that which is personally pleasant to us, and try to dodge that which is unpleasant, even though the unpleasant may be for our real benefit.

But in magical training, we have to try to adopt a more adult attitude, and to realize that it is only by losing this attachment to the pleasant, and by accepting the discipline of sacrifice, that we really progress. It is true, of course, that by sheer force of personal will, we can train ourselves to draw through the cosmic energies; they are pressures which will flow through every channel which is opened for them. However, the result of the passage of these energies through the undisciplined and unregenerate personality is to exaggerate whatever unbalance exists therein, and just as a faulty wire in an electrical circuit may set a house on fire, so the effect of the forces upon the personality can be similarly disastrous. Those who pursue this path of unbalanced development will, if they do not realize their danger in time, join the ranks of those who are termed "Sons of perdition, wandering stars, waves of the sea, foaming out their own shame, fleeing where no man pursueth, for whom is reserved the blackness of darkness for the ages of the ages." However, if you sincerely and constantly reaffirm your desire to serve God and humanity, and carry out the instructions you are given, you have nothing to fear. But you *will* be tested, and the tests will be given you by life itself. You may have read highly romantic accounts of the tests which the neophytes of the Mysteries underwent, but in the actual work, the tests are not so dramatic, though they are none the less quite as effective.

I remember the case of one magical school where the students had to live together in a community and where each student had a small patch of garden which had to be cultivated by him in the periods when the rhythm of training swung from the mental to the physical. It would happen, on occasion, that as the students sat together at lunch and looked out of the window at their gardening efforts, they would see, to their dismay, that one of several animal inhabitants of the school was engaged in wrecking, in a few minutes, the result of weeks of work.

The "test" was to be able to observe this without any resentment or sorrow, since it was taught that non-attachment to results was a sovereign virtue. So it is, but not exactly in that way, and the test became one not of attachment, or non-attachment, but, as Dion Fortune told me when recounting her experiences in this school, as to whether you could acquire a good "poker face". It was, of course, held that the principal could observe clairvoyantly the inner feelings of the students, but the commendations or otherwise which were given, did not appear to substantiate this. All this is not necessary; life itself will apply the tests, and your own inner self will pass judgement upon your reactions to them.

# CHAPTER VII

# THE TREE AS AN INDICATOR

FROM your diary I see that you have been doing quite well in your meditations and in your use of the Tree as a "filing system". You will find that as you use the Tree in this way, that certain *Sephiroth* are easily used while others again do not seem so congenial. You are hereby instructed to pay especial attention to these particular stations, since the fact that they are so difficult or uninteresting is a sure sign that the qualities associated with them are out of balance in your own inner make-up. Possibly they are uncovering old mental repressions and inhibitions, to the dismay of your subconscious mental levels.

Apart from this, however, you are doing quite well, and are ready for the next part of the exercise. But a certain amount of careful study is necessary before this can be used by you; it is in this connection that I want to give you the principles upon which further development is based. Your work with the symbols of the Tree has begun to associate certain happenings in the outer world with the attributes of these various symbols, and they are now becoming "charged" with mental and emotional meaning. It is only when this has been done, to some extent at least, that the next part of the work can begin, so I want you to regard your work at the present time as falling into two distinct categories. First of all, you are building foundations, and upon the strength and accuracy of these depends the safety of the superstructure you may erect. It is necessary, therefore, that these foundations should be "well and truly laid".

Now your work upon the Tree is a very important part of this foundation work, and only when you have gained the habit of seeing automatically every happening in terms of the Tree, can you be said to have truly laid the foundations of your projected work. You must therefore persevere with the basic work on the Tree of Life, before you can proceed with the second part of the task, namely the practical application of both your inner faculties and your inner powers. As an apprentice you must learn that, however clear your vision of deeper things may be, it is very necessary that you should "gain your skills" by the ancient and honourable process of hard work!

At the same time, hard work does not mean drudgery, and it is no part of the training for me to insist upon you doing monotonous exercises simply for the sake of doing them. So although you must redouble your efforts to link the Tree with life as you experience it, I want to give you some idea of the next step in your training.

First of all, I want you to imagine that you are standing in front of the main switchboard of a great electricity station. Before you are scores of meters, coloured lights, and massive switches. As a stranger to electrical practice, what do all these things mean to you? Here and there you may see a word on a dial or on an instrument which conveys some meaning to you, such a word as "volts", or "overload", or "feeder", but whether these words bear the same meanings that are normally associated with them, you, as a stranger to electrical practice, are unable to judge.

If, therefore, you wish to understand the workings of the switchboard, you must learn something of the underlying theory of electricity, and the same thing holds good in the magical field of operations. Just as, seeing a certain meter needle move down its scale, the switchboard attendant will open this switch or close that, so in the magical work you will direct the power here and there in accordance with the indications which you receive from the mental and psychic switchboard which you have built up. But, and this is the point, you will readily perceive that you are "seeing as in a mirror, imperfectly" and in all psychism this is the case. In both the electrical and psychic switchboards however, the meters do not control the power, they simply indicate its presence and volume. The switches regulate and control it. In the case of the psychic switchboard the same principle applies.

Now the process of magical training is designed to teach you first how to receive the impressions which are coming in constantly from the inner planes, and then how to direct the forces which are being indicated by these impressions into the correct channels. Just as the meters on the board symbolize the energies which are passing through them, so their equivalents, the symbols of the Tree, show forth the cosmic energies which are coming to you.

Or, to change the metaphor, in these symbols which you are being trained to use, you are learning the Alphabet of the Mysteries. When this has been learnt, you will be able to begin to speak in the language of the Mysteries, and in this way to make your own personal contact with the Tradition and with those who stand behind it.

The human mind is not, with certain exceptions, adapted to deal with abstract things, and much of the failure of certain occult schools comes from their endeavours to train their pupils along purely abstract lines. This is as though one attempted to build a lofty structure without the aid of scaffolding. The scaffolding is no part of the permanent building, but without its use, the actual process of construction would be much slower and more difficult. There will come a time when, if you have "made the grade", you will learn to "meditate in the empty shrine", to work without the images, but that time is in the future, and therefore you are given this training in symbolism which will enable you to prepare for that imageless working.

But do not make the mistake which many have made in the past, and which many are still making, of taking the image for the reality which it symbolizes. This is always the trouble in esoteric training, and it is against this that I especially wish to warn you. All the symbolic images, with their wealth of detail and colour, are but the indicators of the invisible forces; they are but the letters of an alphabet and in themselves have no meaning apart from that which they symbolize.

One of the most helpful facts about the system of symbolism which we use, is that it has its roots in the dim and distant past, and that it has been used in this kind of work from time immemorial. This means that, in what C. G. Jung terms the "collective unconscious" the images have been well established by the meditations of the followers of this Tradition throughout the centuries. It follows, therefore, that by meditating on these symbols you will come more easily into psychic contact with the inner forces, than if you were working with an entirely new system. The path has been well trodden and you do not need to make such an effort to establish it yourself.

So for all these reasons, you are trained on the symbol system of the *Qabalistic* Tree of Life. But, as I have told you, do not make the mistake of taking the symbol for that which it represents.

I expect you will be asking me why it is not possible to develop the psychic powers and to see the inner planes, just as, say, the spiritualist develops clairvoyance and is able to see the people and conditions of the other worlds. Here again, the same rule applies. The psychic, looking into the astral world perceives that world under the forms of earthly landscape, and usually asserts that this *is* the nature of that plane. But, as I wrote in my book, the appearances of those levels of the inner planes with which we usually come in contact are the "creations of the created"; they are due to the form building powers of the human mind working upon the plastic matter of the astral light. The real appearances of that world are quite different, and cannot be perceived under earth imagery. In very truth, we see as in a mirror, imperfectly, when we look into those worlds. But this applies equally to the ordinary things here on earth; they also are seen by us in a mirror. If you look at your table what do you see? Not the real table; that which the scientist will tell you is an infinitely complex arrangement of forces, electrons, protons, neutrons, etc., all in rapid motion and whirling in certain predetermined paths, but only that *appearance* which is presented to physical sight.

You will see that the same principle runs through all the planes, and this is a very important point, one indeed, which it is imperative that you should keep in mind throughout all your practical work. Otherwise you will become a slave of the images, instead of their master.

It is a very good exercise in concentration to write down two or three of the Tree symbols and then construct a short story around them, a story in which the characters act in accordance with the symbol which they bear. Thus the symbol for the *Sephirah Geburah* is a red disc, and the "magical image" which is associated with it is the figure of a warrior. In the same way, the *Sephirah Netzach* is indicated by a green disc and its magical image is a beautiful woman.

Don't have too many characters in your little mental play, but keep them moving all the time. The mental images must each have the coloured disc of their appropriate *Sephirah* somewhere on their person. You should make this little play as vivid as you can, and give the emotional tone, the feeling which each figure should carry. This is a very good exercise, for it trains you in the association of the different symbols with the forces which they represent. At a later date, when you do some very important visualizing work, this preliminary exercise will be found to have laid good foundations.

When you have gained some proficiency with this exercise, you will find that it tends to overflow, as it were, into your outer life. You will find yourself automatically associating the people and the conditions around you with the appropriate station and its emotional significance. At first this will be somewhat limited; you will deal with primary colours, as it were, and neglect the various shades in between, but with practice you will find that a more flexible use of the symbols is possible.

All this, of course is, to use our switchboard analogy, learning to read the meters and to understand what their indications mean. Or, if you find our other analogy more to your taste, you are learning to put together the letters of the Alphabet of the Mysteries, and to form simple words. I am giving you these two analogies for a definite reason. First of all, it may be that one or the other is more congenial to your mental type, and this will make it easier for you to understand. The switchboard analogy uses the terms of "form", while the alphabet analogy applies to "life" or "consciousness". You will realize, of course, that I am also indicating to you that it will be as well if you attempt to use, at least occasionally, the analogy which is not so congenial. You will have to balance up at some point in your training, so why not do it in the early stages?

It is necessary to learn to think in a foreign language in order to speak it with any degree of fluency. In other words, the process must become automatic. In the beginning you will laboriously and consciously associate a foreign word with its English equivalent, but with practice there will come a time when the idea which is being expressed, say in French or German, is directly understood without this conscious process of translation. The translation will have become automatic and you will have begun to think in the language concerned.

So in just the same way, your mind works when you are learning the language of the Mysteries. At first you will laboriously associate each symbol with its corresponding happening around you, but with constant practice the association will become automatic, and the symbol will rise in the mind without any conscious effort on your part. But do remember, that this must only happen *when you will it to happen*; the rising up of the symbols must always be kept under the control of the will. It is most important that you should realize and act upon this here, at the beginning of your training. Unless you gain this control over the images, you will have much trouble later on.

Well now, I think I have given you sufficient for the time being. Keep on with these exercises and use your own ingenuity to make them as interesting as possible. Make a game of them, or as I have said, construct small plays around the magical images. If you have any talent for drawing use it in this way, but always remember to associate the figures in the picture with their corresponding emotion.

As I have referred to the artistic element, I am reminded of a little trick which may help you in your visualization work, and which will be most useful to you when you attempt certain telepathic experiments at a later date. If you get a short cardboard or metal tube (about two or three inches in diameter) you can use it in this way. Having drawn your picture or having chosen the station on the Tree which you will use for your exercise, place the picture or drawing on the table and look at it through the tube. You will find that the drawing or picture stands out much more clearly than before, due, of course, to the fact that you have excluded the surrounding images from claiming your attention. You must not, however, get into the habit of relying upon this aid, so in addition to those exercises in which you use this screening tube, you must also perform a similar set without its help.

I think you now have sufficient work to do for quite a long time. As I have told you, this is foundation work, and must not be done in a "slapdash" way. So carry on with the work you have been given, and let me have your diary report in the usual way, together with any queries or comments you may wish to make. By the way, keep a close look-out on the reactions of your wife and your friends to your work in this field. Though they may not be able to see what you are *doing*, they cannot help noting what you are *becoming*, and it is by this that you will be judged. Keep an eye also upon your own reactions to them. It may be that you will find yourself becoming irritable or otherwise emotionally disturbed. If so, remember that the fault will, in the majority of cases, lie with yourself. In some ways you have not been working as you should. Before attempting to blame those around you for these upsets, take a very careful look at your work as recorded in your diary. As the entries will be read by you in cold blood, as it were, you should be able to see where you have gone wrong, and you can then take steps to put things right.

You know Nature always attempts to eject from a living organism anything that is a foreign body within it, and the group mind to which you belong will try to do the same with you as soon as you begin to become different from the mass of those around you. But we are training you to become an integral part of the group mind of your race while at the same time you develop new ways of looking at things, and become capable of transmitting your new point of view by your attitude to life. So do not in any way draw attention to your esoteric studies; such a desire for attention is one of the things you will learn to eliminate from your character. Any indication of the nature of your studies apart, of course from intelligent discussion on the subject generally should be given to those around you through your reactions to life. It has been said that actions speak louder than words, and although this may be a trite Victorian axiom, it is a very true one.

Keep in your racial group mind; don't openly defy it! Leave that to the host of would-be reformers who have not yet learnt to reform themselves, but who claim to have an infallible remedy for all the sin and suffering in the world.

# CHAPTER VIII

## "FANTASY IS THE ASS WHICH CARRIES THE ARK"

I SEE from your diary that you have been having a fair amount of success in your work on the Tree, so I can go a little further with your instruction. I want to teach you the art of projecting the thought images which you have learnt to construct. However, before I go on to this, I have to repeat the warning which I have given you so many times in my instructions. *Never fall into the habit of allowing these thought-images to rise into consciousness unless you have definitely willed them to appear.* You must control the images, not be controlled by them.

Particularly is this the case when you begin this work of image-projection. This process must not be confused with the one which psychologists term "projection" which is an involuntary act of attributing certain values to other people and to things. Thus, the apprentice in magical work may give to the craftsman who is training him a curious authority; he may find himself automatically regarding the craftsman as a very Wise Old Man, and may lean upon his authority as a child upon its father. But this is not healthy, though in the beginning of magical training it is more or less inevitable. After all, the craftsman *does* know, or *should* know, more about magic than the newly joined apprentice. However, the craftsman must always work in such a way that this psychological projection is drawn away from him, and the apprentice must train himself to be independent of the craftsman, for at a later date he will have to do his magical work without his continual help, so why not start to do this at an early stage? You must not think that this gives permission for you to try all kinds of magical experiments on your own. You might find yourself in the position of the sorcerer's apprentice in the old story, and be unable to control the forces you have evoked.

At the beginning of my magical career I projected such values upon my own teacher; he would have had to have been a god in order to measure up to it. Gradually I learnt that, like all teachers, he had feet of clay, and over the years I began to withdraw this projection of values, this identification of him with the archetypal Wise Old One. If, at a later date, you are accepted and become a member of our Fraternity, you will find the same rule being applied. Although you will find the power and help of the brethren behind you when you really need help, you will also find that in the application of that power you must work out your own salvation. Now just as you can project such *values* in an entirely involuntary fashion, so you can project definite *images* by the same method.

Perhaps the most common way in which this happens is in your dream-life. Here images are being projected into consciousness in an involuntary way. You have no control over the dream incidents unless, like Peter Ibbetson, in du Maurier's book, you can "dream true". This particular power of dreaming true is one which you will learn to use, but I am dealing just at present with the normal dream images.

Such images arise in response to underlying energies which are attempting to come into expression in life and they are both an ejection of repressed mental material and an indication of the way which must be trod. The sources of many such dreams can be traced to factors in the mind which are more or less accessible, but there is evidence that there is a deeper level of the mind which is using these dream images in order to bring about true mental growth. This guiding power within can be imaged as the Ancient Wise One, and the authority which you may have projected involuntarily upon your external teacher can be withdrawn and directed to this inner authority.

But I must warn you that even to this inner authority you should not give absolute obedience. Whatever monitions you receive from this inner teacher must be weighed in accordance with your outer conditions, and this judgement must be made by you in *full consciousness*. For, although wisdom may, and does, reside within you, the "baffling and perverting carnal mesh" as Browning describes it, will colour that which passes through it from the deeper levels of the mind.

Now just as you project the mental images in an involuntary manner in the dreams of the night, so there is a positive method whereby you can project them into apparent objective reality, and this power can be used in a variety of ways. I will do my best to describe the way in which you must set to work; like learning to ride a cycle, the essential part must be learnt by attempting to do it and persevering until the power is gained. This means, of course, that I cannot tell you how long it will be before you are able to project the images in this way; it all depends on you.

This power of seeing visions is one which we in these modern days seem to have lost; at least in the positive aspect of the faculty. There is a good deal of involuntary mental projection of both images and values in many of the "occult" and psychic groups, but it is rarely that the positive projection is taught. In former times such a voluntary use of the visualizing faculty was a normal thing.

It exists to-day chiefly among artists, though it often seems to me that some modern art reveals more about the inner mental state of the artist than about whatever subject he may have chosen to use in his painting. However, I may be prejudiced in this matter.

I remember being introduced, many years ago, to a small child who could draw remarkable silhouette pictures. They were wonderfully precise and clear in outline and for a child of six or seven it was a very unusual performance. When I asked her how she could draw sucn accurate outlines, she said, "It's easy. I think, and then I draw a line round my think." She evidently had this power of visual projection as a natural talent, and did not realize that it was not possessed by everyone.

Well, all being equal, if you follow the instruction I am giving you now, you should be able to develop this same power. As to how long it will take to succeed in this exercise I can only repeat what I have said many times before: it all depends on yourself.

The exercise falls into two parts. The first is the definite building up of the mental image you intend to project. This is the hardest part to *do*, just as the knack of getting the image "out of your head" as it were, is the most difficult thing to *acquire*. However, until you have trained yourself to build up definite mental images, it is wasted effort to attempt to acquire the power of projecting them. This is a two-way exercise, you have to learn to "bring the images" as well as to exteriorize them, and this means that some really hard work will be required from you before you have mastered it. It is, however, the foundation of a very great deal of what is to follow, and the more proficient you become in this exercise, the more easily will you manage the more advanced work. I know there are people who apparently develop some of the inner powers without any such training, but unless they do train in this way, their power is not consistently available, neither can they direct it as they should.

And now I want to teach you the first part of the exercise: the bringing in of the image. For this you will need some picture or symbol (any picture will do, your common sense will guide you, and obviously you would not use a picture which tended to lead your thoughts away from the main object of the work).

For preference choose a picture with a good deal of detail. The simple geometric forms should be reserved for later work. This is because the mind tends to jib when forced to attend to only one or two points and this makes the work more difficult. The more detailed picture gives it scope to wander, within limits.

Place your chosen picture on the table in such a way that you can sit and look at it without any strain. Keep the rest of the table clear, except for your symbolic picture or image. If you wish, you can use the cardboard tube I told you about, to screen any other visual impressions. Now look quietly at the picture. Do not strain in any way, but look at it as you would look at any object in the normal way. When you have contemplated it in this way for a minute, begin to analyse it; to see its component parts, and to isolate one from the other, to some extent at least.

It is a good plan to give yourself a running description of the picture, and in the beginning of your work on it, you should make this running commentary in an audible voice, though of course you can keep it low!

Perhaps if I give you an example of how you should go to work it will help you. So we will assume that you have chosen for your picture a simple landscape; say a cottage at the side of a wood, with a man sitting with his dog at the open door. Having quietly looked at it for a minute or so, begin, as I have said, to analyse it like this:

"The background of this picture is a small wood, made up chiefly of beech trees, though here and there the artist has painted in some small oaks. It would seem that the season of the year is autumn, as the leaves of the beech are turning a very lovely brown . . . the whole scene is bathed in mellow sunshine. The beechwood seems to be on the side of a hill, and the cottage nestles in to it at its foot, separated from it, however, by a level stretch of garden, part of which I can see because of the slant of the picture.

"The cottage is white-walled, thatched, with small windows, all of which, in the picture, are open. The man is shown as elderly, bearded, with an appearance of 'heavy relaxation'; he seems to slump in the chair, which is the old-fashioned wheelback type, once very common in such cottages.

"The dog which sits by his side is a black and white collie, and the man sits with his hand on the dog's neck. Dimly seen through the open door are some articles of furniture and from the cottage chimney a curl of smoke ascends lazily into the clear sky."

You will see that not only have I described the picture, but I have also indicated the "atmosphere" which the artist was trying to express in it. The more you can do this, the more you will be able to get "out" of the exercise itself. Also, this practice will help you to develop your powers of observation.

Now we come to the next part. Having analysed the picture you must now "bring in the images", and here you are up against the fact that this is an acquired skill which has to be *caught* by you, not *taught* by me.

Normally one does not analyse one's vision; sufficient it is for us that we see. But the actual process of vision is a very interesting thing and it will repay study. First of all, the rays of light reflected from the object we are looking at are received by the eyes, and focused by the lenses in the eye and thus reach the sensitive screen at the back of the eye which is known as the "retina". Here the visual picture is transformed into nerve impulses which travel along the optic nerves until they reach the vision centre in the back of the brain. Here they are received, and in some way of which we know very little they are interpreted by the mind. This is an entirely subconscious process.

What you have to do is first to accompany, as it were consciously, the incoming images to this receiving centre. This is the first half of the work; in the second half the reverse process must be attempted; that is, you must try to accompany the images back to the eye. This may sound silly, but as an actual technique it works.

So, as you look at your chosen picture dwell on it first of all quietly and without strain, having previously analysed it as I have shown; then turn your attention inwards, closing your eyes but keeping the mental image of it, travelling back into the inner darkness of your head, carrying with you this image, until, in your imagination, it has reached the receiving centre. As I have said this sounds silly, but it is a way of training the visual faculty, and it works. It will help you if you time this withdrawal into the depths with one complete inhalation of breath.

Now as you exhale, travel forward again to the front of the head and, opening the eyes, look again at the picture. Repeat this process about half a dozen times, and at each attempt take a different part of the picture with you. That is, as you look at it, select some one part, say the open door and the man seated by it, for one attempt, and for the next take the cottage in its setting in front of the wood. Then, perhaps, the woods themselves, and so on. You will remember that in my book *The Magician*, I said "Let one form of apprehension *glide on* into the other*." It is this change-over from optical image to mental perception which you must practise, until it becomes familiar.

I dealt fairly fully with this in the chapter on "Visualisation and Audition" in my book, so you should have some idea of this already.

The second part of the exercise is more interesting but until you

* *The Magician*, page 15 et seq.

have mastered (to some extent at least) the first part, your results in projecting the images will be rather poor and sketchy. Of course, you may have the innate faculty which was possessed by the little girl to whom I referred earlier on in this instruction, but as a general rule, such spontaneous power is unusual. Now comes the second part of the exercise. You have to formulate the mental images in the back of the head as it were, then bring them forward to the eyes, and finally throw them outside the head and see them no longer as subjective images, but as definite objective pictures. To do this you must have prepared some surface upon which the images are projected. Any monochrome surface will do for this. I have used a saucer containing find sand which had been smoothed to a level surface; a crystal ball, and a black mirror. I find the confused reflections in a crystal rather distracting and the same is true, to some extent, of the black concave mirror. However, in this matter there is a good deal of variation; some people find one method better than another, much depends upon personal factors. Try the various methods, and use that which you find gives you the best results.

As the magical tradition teaches that you should make your own magical instruments, here is an opportunity to do this. Crystals can be bought, and it is obviously beyond the power of the average person to make one, but the mirror can easily be manufactured, and the saucer of sand or its equivalents can also be easily procured. In this latter method there is considerable scope for the use of the colour symbolism of the Tree by using coloured powders.

To make the concave mirror, first of all obtain one of the concave "watch-glasses" which are used in chemistry and in the manufacture of clocks. The size is immaterial, but in order to avoid any auto-hypnosis at this stage, I would suggest one about three or four inches in diameter. Now paint the *convex* surface with black paint or enamel, and you have your "magic mirror". You may elaborate this, if you wish, and set it in a frame. I have seen one set in a frame with all the signs of the Zodiac upon it, but, this is, to my mind, an unnecessary piece of ornamentation; moreover, it tends to distract your attention. However, if you feel you want it "tuppence coloured", try it, but I would strongly advise you to keep it as plain as possible.

Now let me make one thing quite clear. I am not suggesting for one moment that you should use this mirror for any attempt at "crystal-gazing", by which term I mean a passive gazing at the mirror in the hope of seeing clairvoyant images within it. This is a positive training in visualization, not involuntary psychism. I want to make this perfectly clear, because it may be that you have some latent psychic faculty which could be exteriorized in this way, but I do not want to lead you down a path which, at a later date, you will have to retrace. In the carefully controlled psychism of the magical lodges, you will be able to use whatever psychic faculty you have, but in a positive manner. So do not succumb to the lure of quick results, they are seldom satisfactory.

Having procured, or made, your "speculum" as it is termed, you are ready to begin the second part of the exercise, the projection of the images. Sit with the mirror placed in such a position that you are perfectly comfortable as you gaze at it. There must be no strain and particularly there must be no eye-strain. This is very important, since such a strain could lead to the production of the auto-hypnotic state, a state which we do not wish to produce at this point. I have found that if I place the mirror in the same position as I place a book I am reading this gives satisfactory results. Some people place it in their laps, but again the movement of the body in breathing tends to distract the attention.

Having placed the mirror to your satisfaction you must now look at your picture; bring in the image as you have trained yourself to do, and then reverse the process. The image should be brought forward mentally to the eyes, and then projected on to the surface of the mirror. It is difficult to describe this "projection", it is a mental trick which comes quite suddenly after perhaps dozens of attempts. The best way in which I can put it is that you should bring forward the image as I have told you, and then gaze with quiet expectancy at the surface of the mirror. Do not strain the eyes in any way. If you wish to blink the eyelids, do so; there must be no strain.

As I have said, it may be that for a long time you will practise this without success in projection, and then, quite suddenly, you will see in the dim surface of the mirror some part of the picture. I say some part, because we always tend to use our mental power in a focused manner, as a kind of mental electric torch with which we examine something by moving the focused beam across the object we wish to see. But the broader our mental beam, the more of the picture we shall be able to project on the mirror.

When you find you have begun to have some success in this projection exercise, you can begin to use various objects as starting points, and these projections in three dimensions will train you in the art of visualization "in the round". This, you will remember from my previous instruction, is a splendid practice for the building of thought-forms at a later stage.

I think I have given you enough to do for quite a time. Carry on with this, and record it in your diary. It is a good idea to record first the general results in it, and then to write out a detailed description in an exercise book kept for the purpose. In this you can put down the conditions under which the experiment was carried out: the atmospheric conditions, the absence, or otherwise, of noise and other distractions, and the way in which the picture appeared in the speculum. All this will be of great help to me, and also will give you some idea of the best way to go to work with the exercise.

# CHAPTER IX

# "THE MULTITUDE OF COUNSELLORS"

YOU tell me that you have managed to settle down to your meditation routine, and are beginning to be able to build up fairly good mental pictures. Also, you have obtained a copy of *The Mystical Qabalah.*

Now, however, although you have started your training and are making some progress, you have run into trouble from other quarters, with the result that there is a certain amount of confusion in your mind. You tell me that a friend of yours, deeply interested in esoteric subjects, has warned you against becoming involved in any practical work, save that of meditation; he has also made your flesh creep with stories of the dangers of what he terms "the lower psychism". On the other hand, another friend, this time an ardent spiritualist, has extolled the virtues of the "developing circle" where, he says, without any arduous meditation or other mental work, you would be able to develop your innate psychic powers which would bring you into contact with "true spiritual guides". Yet again, a medical acquaintance has warned of the dangers of "trance" and "split personality". Finally, your parish priest, who has been told of your interests, has given you stern warning against "dabbling with these unholy things".

You certainly seem to have a multitude of counsellors, but whether in this there is safety, remains to be seen. You may remember the story of the man who tried to follow out all the advice given by those whom he met while riding his donkey. He ended, you will remember, by *carrying the donkey* into town, to the great amusement of the townspeople!

Seriously though, I have been expecting this situation to develop. It usually comes along when the training has definitely started, and before any striking success has been achieved. This again is a test of your ability to go ahead on your chosen path without being swayed by the opinions of others. The outcome rests with yourself, but as you have referred the situation to me, as your teacher, I will try to give you some guidance.

First of all, let me suggest that all this advice which has been so kindly proffered has some value, even though some parts may seem to cancel out others. There is always something to be gained from the ideas of others, even though it may be thought that such ideas are ill-informed or even due to bigotry. We are all liable to this latter fault, it is not peculiar to parsons, doctors and teachers can be just as fixed in their ideas as any religious leader.

I will take each of these warnings separately, and in the same order as you give them in your letter. First of all let us consider the question of what your friend calls the "lower psychism". As you will be aware, you have two great systems of nerves in your body: the voluntary and the involuntary systems. The involuntary system is the older of the two, and it governs the whole of what may be termed the automatic processes of the body, such as breathing, digestion, and all the multitude of activities which go on within you.

The other, the voluntary or cerebro-spinal system, is of a more recent evolution, and is the medium of expression of your conscious waking self. But, it is also dependent upon the older system of nerves, and the type of consciousness which goes with it, for its successful operation. Thus, you lift your arm by an act of will. But the whole complex activity of nerve and muscle, of variation in blood flow, of the discharge of energy along the nerve paths, and the intricate mechanism by which that energy makes the muscles move in the way you wish; all this is effected by the involuntary system, *working under the direction of the voluntary consciousness.*

But just as there is a form of consciousness (the waking consciousness) which is expressed through the cerebro-spinal system, so there is also a form of consciousness which works through the involuntary nerves, and this is usually referred to as the "sub-conscious" or "subliminal" mind. As this subliminal part of the mind is the product of ages of evolution from the very remote past, it has, of necessity, very primitive aspects which reflect the primitive consciousness of those early days. It is, however, also linked with that part of our whole consciousness which lives on the inner planes, and *all* psychic experiences, whether "high" or "low", are transmitted to the waking self *through* the subliminal levels of the mind. You will remember that we discussed, in a previous instruction, the *chakras* or psychic centres. Well, these psychic centres are linked with certain points in the involuntary nervous system, and can transmit their impressions by way of the corresponding aspect of the subconscious which is expressed in those parts of that system. But, just as you can cause your arm to move at your will and perform some particular operation, so the subconscious levels of the mind can move your arm *without* your willed intention. So, for instance, you may write something which has been carefully composed by you in your everyday waking state, and all the subconscious mechanisms move your muscles to make letters and words of the necessary size and form, and arrange the resultant words in their correct grammatical order; all these activities have become what we call a "habit", which is the result of our mental training. However, this mental machinery can run itself without your conscious will, and then we get the phenomenon of what is usually called "automatic writing". The dreams of the night are examples of what might be termed "automatic seeing", and all the sense activities of the body can work in reverse, as it were, in this way.

Usually, the results of such reverse working are not very helpful. They consist, for the greater part, of material which is the accumulation of many years of mental activity, both good and not so good, and although such material may be of interest to the psychiatrist, it is not in itself of any value, except as an indication of the mental processes that are going on down below in the depths of the mind.

But, mixed with this subconscious outpouring, we find evidences of psychic activity, though they are like the grains of gold in the gold-bearing quartz rock, few and far between. This welling up of the psychic perception and action through the activity of the subliminal levels of the mind is termed, in your friend's philosophy, the "lower psychism". His objection to it, and it is an objection which is made by all the occult and esoteric schools, is that it is a reversion to the past of evolutionary time. It is the revival of the primitive mirror psychism which is still to be found in the higher animals, such as cats, dogs, and horses, and because it is not under the control of the conscious mind, it can lead to the dissociation and personality splitting against which your medical friend warns you.

However, though I do not wish to develop you as an involuntary psychic, there are some criticisms which I can make with regard to this objection. First of all, with very few exceptions, the "positive" voluntary psychism is rare, and even when it has been developed, the psychic has his "off-days", and ill-health or mental and emotional stress will distort his perceptions.

Most psychics occupy positions along the scale from pure "positive" to pure "negative", and move one way or the other according to the prevailing conditions. In addition to this, the negative psychism can, under certain conditions, be changed over to the positive variety, though in the majority of cases, psychics of the involuntary type find their powers vanish when they begin to do the meditation work required of them by the magical and esoteric schools. This is because of the increased activity of the cerebro-spinal system along new and unfamiliar lines, and it usually discourages such people as they feel that they are losing something of value. However, if they persevere with their training, they find that the faculty returns and is capable of being used in a more effective way.

But I do want to remind you that the magical schools are not for psychic development. It is true that psychic faculties are exercised in the lodges, and their use does play a part in the work on which they are engaged. But the primary purpose of the magical training is the mental and spiritual unfoldment of the members, and psychism is regarded as a means to an end, and not in any sense as an end in itself.

Now let me comment on the objections of your medical friend. It is quite true that *certain forms* of *psychic* activity can lead to the mental troubles to which he refers, but as a general rule, this danger is not so great as it might seem. If we are dealing with any subject we tend to see it all around us, we are mentally looking for its appearance, and are often rather disappointed if we fail to find it. So the specialist is on the look-out for the manifestations of his particular speciality, the religious zealot has conditioned himself to see the weaknesses and transgressions of his fellow men, and politicians are always putting the world to rights according to their own infallible prescriptions.

However, when we try to find out what effect the psychic faculties may have upon their possessors, we must find out what was the state of their general mental health before they started development. As you will have read in my books there are people who are suffering from slight mental dissociation, who "see" imaginary things, or "hear" imaginary voices, and this of course is a sign of definite mental illness. Should such people be allowed to enter the ordinary "developing circle", or be encouraged in some magical school to induce certain mental states, then the illness of the mind from which they are already suffering will develop until finally a complete mental breakdown ensues. Here of course, the issue is simple. In many cases, however, the breakdown is not complete, the visions and voices do not take the sufferer right out of everyday reality, though they do very considerably affect his life and conduct. It is these "half-way" people, who are the curse of the psychic movements, and who bring upon them the strictures of the medical psychologists.

But, as you will see, everything depends upon those who are leading the movements or schools concerned, and it is for this reason that I have asked you to observe the character and general mental outlook of any school you were thinking of entering. For the lives and characters of those who have been trained in any school give you a good indication of its value.

I should like to give you my own ideas on this question of the mental unbalance in the psychic and esoteric schools. During a period of some forty-five years of actual contact with both occult and psychic movements, I have met men and women of all mental levels, and have observed that mental unbalance is by no means confined to psychics. There are, as I have said, some who do display such unbalance, but on investigation it is usually found that the signs of such mental trouble were there some time before they started their "development". Blame, of course is to be attached to the so-called leaders of such circles, but it is evident that the fault as a general rule lies with the person, not the system.

Exactly the same criticism applies to those who are members of the esoteric schools. Though many of them loftily regard their psychic brethren as victims of the lower psychism, the fact remains that some of them display just the same symptoms of mental unbalance. I may say in passing, that I have on many occasions heard "spiritualistic seances" heartily condemned by people whom I have later been amused to see furtively paying for a "sitting" with some noted psychic!

Let us be fair. We all fall short of the ideal, and none of us can afford to make stern judgement, even upon ourselves. As Bishop Butler said, as he watched a condemned man being taken to execution, "There but for the grace of God go I." The aim of the magical schools is to integrate more fully the personalities of their apprentices, but one hundred per cent success cannot be guaranteed.

Now I want to deal with the claim of your spiritualist friend.

Whatever may be the merits or demerits of the modern spiritualist movement, one thing is very certain, and that is that the methods and contacts of the usual "developing circle" are not suitable for those who wish to tread High Magic's Way. This is not to condemn spiritualism, which has its part to play in the religious evolution of man, and which, for those who are working in it with serious intent, is as true a path to the light as any other. But "no man can serve two masters", and the methods of spiritualism and those of the magical training schools are not compatible. Until you are able to judge with knowledge, you should follow the methods of training which I am outlining to you, and leave other lines of work to other people.

You must make up your mind on this matter, and let me know your decision. Here, in the very beginning of your magical apprenticeship, comes a test of your possession of that most essential mental virtue, discrimination.

I will finish this part of your instruction with a word or two about

the attitude of your parish priest. There are many like him, unfortunately, but their main trouble is that they have not the slightest idea
of the true nature of magic. They may have the usual concept of
mediaeval magical work, and may even be authorities on the subject
of the various magical rites practised in those times. But their reaction to the whole subject is to regard it as unwholesome, and one
which must be condemned. But the idiocies of the black mass, and
the popularity of the various erotic magical recipes were not part of
the true magic in those days, any more than they are to-day.

On behalf of the priests, however, you must remember that one of
their duties as ordained priests of the Church is, as the Ordinal puts
it, ". . . with all faithful diligence to banish and drive away all
erroneous and strange doctrines contrary to God's Word, and to use
both publick and private monitions . . . as need shall require and
occasion shall be given." This is part of a question put to the ordi-
nand, to which he replies, "I will, the Lord being my helper."

If a priest who knows only of the parodies which go by the name of
magic is confronted with someone like yourself, then he can do only
one of two things. Either he condemns the whole thing, and remem-
bering his vow does his best to "banish and drive away this erroneous
and strange doctrine", or else he refrains from such condemnation
until he has thoroughly studied the subject. But this second line of
action takes quite an effort. He is usually fully occupied with his
work as a parish priest (the fable of the idleness of the parson, though
it still persists among the less informed, *is* in the great majority of
cases just a fable), and it may not be possible for him to make a deep
study of the subject.

Or perhaps there is a definite reason for his opposition which arises
from some experience of his own, or of others whom he has known,
and this may well cause him to regard the whole subject as Satanic.
If you have ever seen the phenomenon of "possession", as many
missionaries have done, then you could understand this wholesale
condemnation.

But more usually, he shrinks from the study of these things because
of theological training and also because he fears the possible reactions of his own flock, and this latter is a very real consideration.

There are many priests and ministers who do not condemn these
things, but who try to understand them in the light of Christian experience. After all the Bible abounds with examples of psychic and
magical happenings and the ceremonies of the Church are a very
potent form of magic, as Evelyn Underhill pointed out in her book
on mysticism.

So do not be unduly annoyed at the attitude of your vicar, thank him for his advice, but assure him the matter is not as he thinks. Then get on with your training; and keep your mouth shut about these things.

You know the magical axiom: "Know, Will, Dare, and *Keep Silent*." Then follow it out. One of the main reasons why this secrecy is asked of you is that you will later be working with thought-forces, and you will not wish antagonistic thoughts of others to break down what you are building up. Also, although it may be that in the multitude of counsellors there may be safety, there is liable also to be much confusion. The "back-seat driver" is just as much a menace in magic as in motoring!

# CHAPTER X

## "GOING OUT AND COMING IN"

AS you now seem able to project mental images at will, I want to give you the basic instruction for accomplishing what is commonly called "astral projection". This means that you actually project a carefully built thought-form and then by a certain mental "trick", locate your consciousness in the projected form.

The form which you build up in this way is known among us as the "Body of Light". In certain eastern books it is termed the *Manumayakosha*, a name which may be literally translated as "the thought-created sheath or body of illusion". I have met many people who either by training or natural aptitude, have possessed this power to project consciousness in an external form. Those who are trained, do it in a somewhat different manner, by a positive "splitting of the Moon", from those who possess that peculiar make-up of the etheric or vital body, which is the basis of the physical manifestations produced through those people who are known in spiritualism as materializing mediums.

The peculiarity of the etheric double of the materialization medium is that the connection with its material counterpart is a loose one, and under certain conditions it may be extruded therefrom. Actually, as it is the mould upon which the physical body is built, total projection of the vital body would mean death. However, this is what is called a "fluidic" body, and can be caused to divide, as it were, a certain minimum amount always remaining with the physical body. By a very wonderful process the vital body when exteriorized in this way, can draw actual material matter from the body and build itself up in a form which is quite perceptible to ordinary sight.

In the materialization seances of the spiritualists the process is done without the medium understanding or in any way directing the process. It is then understood that the projection is due to the activity of discarnate people who mould the projected matter into the appearance of their own former material body. That this may be so in some cases I am firmly convinced from my own experiences in this field, but in many cases it is not necessary to suppose that the spirits of the dead have anything to do with it. In any case, whether we are wearing the earthly overcoat, or have thrown it off (either temporarily or permanently) we are, as we have ever been, spiritual beings. Tennyson in one of his poems refers to the "Ghost in Man" which is meeting with "the Ghost which once was Man". Always remember that you are just as much a spiritual being now as ever you will be through all the ages of eternity.

But to return to our astral projection. It is one of the greatest experiences which come to you when you begin to work on this magical path. To stand in the room, and look at your own physical body lying deep in sleep, is something which gives to you an absolute conviction that, in spite of all the materialistic philosophers may say, you are something more than that body; that you are a being which is independent of that body and capable of existing apart from it.

I well remember, after forty years and more, the wonder and exhilaration I experienced when first I stood forth in the Body of Light.

At the same time, there are certain drawbacks and dangers which I want to explain to you before I give you the instruction which will help you to achieve this wonderful feat. I am telling you of these dangers in order that you may have a clear mental picture of the process right from the beginning of your work along this particular line. It is in ignorance that fear is conceived and fear is the greatest hindrance to success in magical work. If you know the pitfalls, then you can proceed with confidence, but if you walk in ignorance, then will your uninformed imagination people the unseen world with fantastic figures of dread. Again using the idea of balanced activity which is implicit in the *Qobalistic* philosophy, *caution* on the Pillar of Force, and *confidence* on the Pillar of Form provide the balancing opposites which enable you to "travel in the Light".

There are two forms of astral projection, and I want to point out to you the essential difference between them. One is entirely involuntary and not in any way under the control of the person concerned. Here again, much depends upon whether the "projector" slips out of his own accord, or whether he is sent out by the power of another. In my own first successful astral flight, I was assisted by the power of my own teacher, and this is so in very many cases where random experiments are being carried out by those who have gained their instruction from one or other of the many books which touch upon these subjects.

Where the teacher knows what he is about this help can be very effective, but the experiments must not stop at this purely passive projection, lest an unhealthy dependence upon him be built up. In any case, when once you enter the lodge, you will be required to pledge yourself not to allow any control of your will by another person.

The second type of projection is where the person concerned voluntarily steps out from the physical body. This is a more difficult feat, but it has the advantage that the operation is under his own control. There is an intermediate class of projection where the power to step out of the physical body suddenly appears, usually to the dismay and fear of the projector. In these cases the sudden appearance of this power may be due to the welling up from the deeper mind of memories of occult training in previous lives, but in many cases it is due to ill-health, or certain psychic conditions surrounding and affecting the person to whom the experience comes. Which cause is operating in any given case is a matter for experts, *who in these cases are men and women to whom this experience is a commonplace occurrence.* So much nonsense has been foisted upon the public by so-called "experts", doctors, psychiatrists, and orthodox parsons, that those of us who have been working in these fields for many years, have ceased to worry about the opinion of those who attempt to lay down the law on subjects of which they have had no actual experience. So do not worry about the opinions of Dr "X" or Bishop "Y", or for the matter of that, the opinions of the chap on the next bench who jeers at the whole subject. "The laughter of fools is as the crackling of the thorns beneath a pot," says the Bible. If you have ever tried to use the desert thorns as fuel for cooking you will realize the point of this. There is a lot of flame and noise, but very little effective heat.

There are really only two dangers in the practise of "astral projection" in full consciousness. One, which is purely physical, is the possibility of strain upon the heart. The heart is a very tough organ and can stand far more strain than many people realize, but it *can* be tried beyond its limits and will suffer accordingly. Now generalizations are dangerous, but broadly speaking, if you have any kind of heart weakness or abnormality, then the usual methods of projection are not for you, and you will be wise to realize the fact. There are other ways of achieving the same end, but they are slower in their action. Nevertheless, they are just as effective. As a matter of fact, I shall be giving you some preliminary instruction along these other lines very shortly.

The second danger is that the wonder of these experiences may lead you to attempt to escape the woes and worries of this mundane plane by retreating to the Inner Planes whenever the storms of life become a bit boisterous, and this may lead to a pathological mental condition which will bring you into the legitimate sphere of the "expert" psychiatrist. This, however, can only happen if your basic philosophy has been built up on the wrong premises.

You have been taught the *Qabalistic* philosophy, and you know that this philosophy teaches the necessity of leading a full life on this physical plane and of evading none of the duties that are part of it. Brief refreshment after labour is permissible, but extended holidays on the inner levels are not in the plan.

Now in your case, the two main dangers do not seem to me to be liable to cause trouble. Your physical health is good, your heart is sound, and you are sufficiently "down to earth" to be immune from any threat of psychological escapism. We can therefore go ahead with the instructions which will enable you to step forth from this apparently solid flesh in full consciousness.

Again, I want to warn you that success in this branch of magical work depends upon steady and sustained practice. Any desultory work along these lines is doomed to failure. You must persevere with the exercises without setting a time limit to your perseverance. It may be that almost immediately you will be able to step forth in full consciousness, or it may take weeks, months, or even years, before success is yours. But whatever time you take, remember that the actual exercises are also valuable aids to visualization and concentration, apart from their actual objective.

It has suddenly occurred to me that you will have begun to wonder whether there is time in the working day for you to carry out all the instructions I have given you. I remember thinking something like this myself, when I first started my magical apprenticeship. But in point of fact "things are not always what they seem", and it is not as bad as this. As you begin to master the early exercises, you will find that the time necessary for success becomes less and less, until what formerly involved ten minutes or so, now only takes half a minute, since the subconscious mind has begun to form an automatic habit, and the exercises themselves are beginning to produce the necessary developments in the inner body. But in these matters time, as we experience it down here, matters less than we think. You are not being "crammed" for an examination which will take place on a certain fixed date, but are being given an apprenticeship which will merge into craftsmanship when you have gained the necessary proficiency, and not before.

Since it is an apprenticeship it follows that long before you reach the end of it, you will be doing quite a lot of practical work, and what is more, your work will be taken up into the great plan and be used by those master craftsmen with whom and under whom we all serve.

Now let us return to the actual instructions for the projection of the "body of light" as it is called in our school. The best time for this projection, as far as you are concerned, is before you go to sleep. But it will be well to attempt it also at certain other times of the day; this, of course, will be conditioned by your daily routine of work. It is well to remember, however, when you start your attempts at projection, to tell your wife what you are going to do, and impress upon her that it would not be helpful if she were suddenly to disturb you!

Your training in the building up of "thought forms" now comes into practice. You have to build up in your mental vision a thought-form which will act as the mould upon which the fluidic "etheric" substance will flow, and so provide the link between the physical and super-physical levels of consciousness. What shape this form should take is very largely a matter for your own choice. I started my projection experiments by building a thought-form of a figure in a deep blue robe with a cowl over the head, a silver girdle round the waist, and, supported by a fine chain, a rather ornate Rosicrucian Cross. However, I was at that time a great admirer of the books of the late Marie Corelli, hence the form I built was directly inspired by a passage in one of them. I remember that my teacher was mildly amused by my choice, but he did not raise any objection. As a matter of fact, you can make this thought-form as you wish, avoiding of course, any grotesque or unsuitable form.

I would suggest that you formulate such a figure as I have described, though you need not follow my pattern exactly. As you will find later on in your magical work, you are already a member of a group composed of both incarnate and discarnate people, and this group is working always on the inner planes. As it is a group using ceremonial, it has its own particular "uniform", and when once you have linked up with this group in full consciousness, whether through your own personal powers or through the psychic faculties of another, then you will know what is the correct form to build in your own particular case.

The appearance of your thought-form having been fixed, you can now proceed to build and project it in the same way as you have trained yourself, to project such forms. I found it very helpful, in the early stages of my training, to project the form in this way. I would first visualize and project a form which was a sphere of deep blue light about the size of an orange. When I had done this successfully I made it expand rapidly and take shape and size. At the conclusion of the exercise I would then reverse this process, and finally draw this ball of light back into myself.

Remember, *this* is *not* the actual Body of Light which you are attempting to project. It is only the form, the mould, into which that fluidic body will flow. You will remember that I have told you of the work which goes on in the "materialization seances", where the etheric substance flowing from the medium, is organized into recognizable forms by the thoughts of both incarnate and discarnate people. Here you are doing the work of both parties. You are supplying the material, and are also building the form into which that material may be built. At the same time you must remember that you are not attempting to project a form which will be visible to ordinary physical eyesight; this is a further development which can be left until you have received further training. As a matter of fact, it is not often attempted since it can only be done by those who have the particular etheric make-up to which I have previously referred. In any case, although it is a very wonderful feat it is not necessary for you to project such a visible form. The finer grade of etheric substance which you will use, is quite sufficient for the work you will be doing.

Now you are ready for the actual attempt at projection. The method I am going to describe is that which I used when I was being trained, and I can vouch for its effectiveness. What I cannot vouch for is the time you will need before you are successful. So much depends upon other factors; it may be only a few weeks or it may be a matter of months or even years. One man whom I knew took seven years to achieve success in this operation. He was exceptional, however. At the same time he displayed an amount of perseverance which was an object lesson to all of us.

The first part of this method of projection has been the building up of the form, and you now have this form standing before you. Your job is to transfer what is sometimes known as the "star of consciousness"; that point within you where you feel yourself to be "I". With most people this point of self-consciousness is located in a vague fashion somewhere behind the root of the nose, but with certain other types it is located in the solar plexus. This latter position is not so common among those who come for training in the western schools, though it does occur in some who are of Celtic blood. But wherever the star of consciousness is located, it has to be transferred to the form you have built. You have also to transfer to the form some of the finer etheric substance of your own vital body; you have to breathe into the form the "breath of life".

As you sit quietly contemplating the form you have built, breathe in a full breath, at the same time direct your attention to the ground beneath your feet, or, if you are lying upon your back, direct it to a point just beyond the soles of your feet. This is actually the earth-contact of your aura, the point where certain etheric energies flow into you from the planetary etheric levels.

So, as you breathe a full charge of air into your lungs, mentally draw up at the same time a full charge of energy from the earth centre, and bring this energy up to wherever you locate your star of consciousness. Then, as you exhale the breath, project the etheric energy out to the form you have built, at the same time endeavouring to go with the stream of force, riding upon it as it were, into the projected form. It will help if you picture a kind of psychic cord linking you with it, and project both the etheric energy and your consciousness along this cord. In this way you are conforming to the etheric "anatomy", since there is such a link between the vital body and its dense counterpart.

You may have to repeat this part of the exercise many times before you have any success, or it may be that almost at once you will find yourself in full consciousness in the Body of Light. But whether it takes a long time or otherwise, it is well worth working for. What usually happens when success has been achieved, is that you are so surprised that you "panic" and bolt back into the safety of the physical body like a young rabbit into its burrow. You are, however, in no danger and if you can only hold on for a moment you will suddenly experience something which will, as it were, anchor you on the etheric levels. With some it is a curious kind of "click", something like the sound of an electric light switch being turned off. With others it may take the form of a musical note which suddenly sounds in the head and this indicates that you are now out of the body in full consciousness.

You will now begin to perceive the actuality of the psychic umbilical cord which links you with the physical form which you have left for a time. You will find that it tends to draw you back into the body and it is best to get a good distance away. You will notice, too, that the nearer to the body you are the thicker the "silver cord" becomes, and the stronger the attraction of the physical. You will find too, that you are, as it were, swimming in some subtle etheric "sea", amid swirling currents of energy, but you will find that you have the power to resist such forces and to maintain your balance.

Experiences vary with the individual, but in my own projections I have always found myself in a realm where the ordinary physical objects were distinctly visible in a bluish light. One peculiarity of this illumination is that it casts no shadows and the effect is rather strange until one becomes used to it.

There will be, you will find, a strong inclination on your part forthwith to visit some friend on the earth, or else to meet someone who has passed from physical life, but for the time being I would counsel you to confine yourself to the task of getting out of the body in full consciousness. Later on you can try to travel in this etheric world, but what you are now doing is simply the preliminary work and it is this which is so important.

If now, having successfully projected in the Body of Light, you wish to return into the physical (and in your early experiments you should make only brief projections), all that is necessary, is for you to approach the physical body. Immediately the silver chord will begin to exert an increasingly powerful pull and you will be drawn rapidly back into physical plane consciousness.

When you are back in the body it is advisable to write down *at once* your recollections of the experience. If you wait for any length of time, you will find the memory has become dimmed.

Now for two warnings and one bit of encouragement. Never try these projection experiments during the period of the waning moon, the etheric currents are not favourable, and although at a later stage you will be able to master them, they can hinder your first attempts. My second warning is keep strict silence during these experiments. You will have quite enough to do in getting out of the physical without being impeded by the antagonistic thought influences of others who know nothing of the subject, but who, nevertheless, either deny it or strongly disapprove of it. Remember the last part of the Rosicrucian motto ". . . keep silent".

Now the encouragement. Although you may feel alone and rather forlorn as you first stand in the Body of Light, believe me when I tell you that you will not be alone. There will be others who are very near to you and ready to help you. Indeed, this is always the case, whatever plane of life we are inhabiting. As Marcus Aurelius wrote so long ago, "We are never less alone than when we think we are alone."

On this note I will end this very important part of these instructions.

I want you to let me have the record of your experiments along this line in the usual way. Please note the following points:

(1) Date and time of experiment.
(2) Your own physical and mental conditions.
(3) The weather conditions.
(4) Any other points which seem to you to be relevant to the experiment.

# CHAPTER XI

# THE CONTACT OF POWER

IN this instruction I want to show you how to make contact with, and draw into yourself, the energies with which you will later be working in the lodge. It is important that you should not only have a clear idea of these energies and their origin, but also that you should be able, in some measure at least, to make contact with them.

As a general rule, the lodge does not like to deal with neophytes who have contacted the energies in a haphazard fashion, since it then falls to the lot of the teacher to break down the faulty habits which have been built up, and to train the apprentice in the methods used in actual magical work.

In your own case, I am trying to establish these good habits *before* you enter the door of the Mysteries, and that which I am now going to give you is a safe, practical, and, given perseverance and aptitude on your part, effective method of making contact with the energies which you will learn to use in the lodge.

The first thing which I must impress upon you is that as far as you are concerned, these energies are entirely "neutral". They can be used for good or evil purposes, and this, of course, applies to *all* natural forces. So do not think in terms of "spiritual forces". They *are* truly spiritual forces, but so are all natural energies whether they operate on the physical or the superphysical planes. All depends upon the use which is made of them, and here we come to the root of the moral teaching of this school.

So much is regarded as moral and spiritual teaching which in reality is nothing of the sort, and it is here that the "first virtue of the Path", as it has been termed, is so very important. This virtue of "discrimination" is your protection against the wrong application of these powers by yourself or by others.

What do we mean by the term "moral"? What do you understand by the word? I am not a betting man, but I would be willing to make a wager that the first idea that arises in your mind when you hear the word is something to do with sex. Am I not right? This is because the true meaning of the word has been limited in common use to this narrow definition. But it is not because the general use of the term is an incorrect one that you should accept its application, indeed, it is imperative that you should learn to use the word in a much larger context.

The general meaning of the word is something to do with the tribal customs. Certain things were good for the tribe as a whole, and were enforced by chief and priest for the common good. The trouble was that as the community grew both in numbers and intelligence, the "mores", the tribal customs, began to be more difficult to apply, and in every age there was some form of revolt against the rigidity of the "moral" code.

Now, although we like to think that we are in every way superior to our forefathers, the sad truth is that we are in many ways just as limited as they were. Although great efforts have been made, and with some success, to bring a really enlightened attitude of mind to bear upon such age-old problems as juvenile delinquency, prostitution, and homosexuality, we are still bogged down by the intricate legal system which has been evolved down the ages, and which both church and state have enforced upon us.

There are signs that the discontent which seeths underneath present-day society will find vent in aggressive action, and this means that every step, however justified, towards a more enlightened application of the Law, will be fiercely resisted by those in Church and State who feel that only in the preservation of the *status quo* is there any security. This fear of new things is characteristic of many of us, but in magic we are taught that in very truth, "The old order changeth, yielding place to new, and God fulfils himself in many ways, lest one good custom should corrupt the world."

This is not to say that we advocate any wholesale breaking down of the moral and legal codes which, on the whole, have served very well, for there is a great deal of sanctified commonsense in the English Common Law. But it does mean that we must use a different measure to that used by our fellow citizens.

If you will look at the Ten Commandments which are regarded as standards in this matter, you will notice that they are all *negative* statements. "Thou shalt not" is their keynote. In the Hebrew nation before the time of our Lord, there had been many attempts to put out a more positive teaching, and He, as a master psychologist, took some of these earlier ideas and summed them up in the two *positive* commandments which both begin with "Thou shalt". He added also another positive commandment, "That ye love one another".

Study these true expressions of the moral law and you will see that they are real spiritual dynamite, calculated to bring down the walls of many legal and ecclesiastical Jerichos. But be careful not to twist the commandment to suit the case. It is the case which must be altered, and here is one in point! A famous (or to many people an infamous) occultist and magician used as his slogan this statement, "Do what thou wilt shall be the whole of the Law. Love is the law, love under will."

It is the same idea as that expressed by St Augustine: "Love, and do as thou wilt." But, as the late Mr Joad would have said, "What do you mean by *love*?"

In actual practice it resulted in forms of conduct which undoubtedly resulted in misery and suffering for many of those who tried to put this maxim into practice.

The Greeks had a saying which gives one aspect of our magical attitude in these matters. It is *medan edan*, which means "Nothing too much". In our understanding it signifies "balance", and in the magical schools it is said that "equilibrium is the basis of the Great Work". In fact, we refer to the "evil" forces as the "Kings of Edom, the Lords of Unbalanced Force".

But I want you to note that this condition of balance is not a purely static attitude of the mind, something like the "balance" which the artist sometimes strives after: the balance of "still life", the grouping into a pattern. Rather is it the balance of the trapeze artist which is a kinetic balance, due to the employment of complementary forces. So your attitude towards life must be one of flexibility, but a flexibility which is based upon the rock of true morality as opposed to established custom.

But beware of making of your attempts to follow this path an exhibition which will bring you into headlong collision with established custom. In any case this will be a waste of energy which, although it may gratify a masochistic strain in yourself, will not help you in your chosen work.

I am stressing this now, because as soon as you begin to get results from the exercises I am about to describe, you will find that the energies which begin to flow into your being will need careful handling, and it is here that you will find the foregoing moral instruction of value.

These forces which will find their channel through your mind must always be regarded as divine in their origin and nature. The exercises which will bring through these energies are known as the exercises of the Middle Pillar. If you will look at the diagram of the Tree of Life, you will see that there are three vertical lines of the *Sephiroth*: the stations on the tree. The middle vertical line which passes through *Malkuth, Yesod, Tiphareth, Daath*, and *Kether*, is the Middle Pillar, and you will notice that all the stations on this line are connected with the consciousness aspect of your own self. *Malkuth* deals with the physical sensory consciousness; *Yesod* with what is termed the "subconsciousness", or "personal unconscious"; *Tiphareth* is the sphere of superconsciousness; and *Daath* is the point where another order of awareness operates. Finally in *Kether* we have the unconditioned consciousness of the divine spark which is the centre and source of our existence.

Hence I warn you against a very common error. Many apprentices, having followed the instructions and awakened the energies, talk very boastfully of their contact with "*nirvanic* levels". According to the eastern teachings, from which this term is derived, *nirvana* is the state of consciousness where we pass from this planetary and conditioned state of being into one of unconditioned being.

A very necessary corrective to the tendency of overrating personal achievements along this line, is to remember that, according to the *Qabalistic* teaching, there is "a Tree in every *sephira*". Thus, in *Malkuth* all the other *Sephiroth* are experienced, but "through and under the veil of earthly things". The experience of the form of consciousness of *Kether*, through this earthly veil, is a very wonderful experience, but it is *not* the full undistorted consciousness, which belongs only to those who may legitimately be termed masters of life.

This is by way of discouraging any tendency on your part to what the Greeks called *hubris*, the strange spiritual pride and arrogance which so easily arises when the mighty forces of the unseen universe begin to find their channels through our personality.

I have given the exercises in my book *The Magician*, so you will already be familiar with them, but I want to go over them again so that you may understand them more fully.

First of all, remember that you are, as it were, a conducting channel for the forces which flow from two sources, and you have within your psycho-physical make-up the necessary contact points or terminals where these energies may be picked up. There is, in point of fact, an anatomy of the inner bodies (they have their organs, even as the physical body) and in this anatomy there are two terminal centres or *chakras* with which you are primarily concerned in these exercises. They are the centre in the aura just above the head, and the corresponding centre in the aura just below the feet. On the Tree, these two centres are referred to as *Kether* and *Malkuth* respectively.

It is through these two terminals, or centres, that we draw in the energies which we are going to use in our work, and this is how it is done. First of all you must visualize a sphere of pure white radiance about three or four inches above your head. Your training in visualizing and projecting images will have enabled you to do this fairly easily. This radiant sphere of light should be seen as clearly as you can possibly build it up, and at the same time you should "feel" it as a *warm* vibrant globe, charged with power which is steadily being radiated into your aura, travelling down to the earth centre below the feet.

When you have successfully built up this contact point above the head, you must now build up the corresponding terminal below the feet. Again visualize a globe of light, and project and "locate" it about three or four inches below the feet. But instead of the pure white brilliance of the head centre, you must picture the in-coming energy in this earth terminal to be a seething, surging energy of citrine, russet olive, and indigo colours all mixed together in a swirl of colour. As you will see, the visualization of the centre in *Malkuth* is a good deal more difficult than the building up of the *Kether* centre above the head, but it is most important that it should be done.

There has been a good deal of misunderstanding about this basic centre. Many people have said that if you wear rubber shoes you will cut yourself off from the "earth magnetism", as it is called. This is not the case unless you make it so by definitely forming the idea that you will insulate yourself in this way. We are all living in the etheric counterpart of this planet. We are, in fact, immersed in it as a fish in the ocean. So, to imagine that the barrier of half an inch of rubber will prevent the etheric energies reaching us, is foolish. At the same time, there *are* certain forces which radiate from the ground on which we walk, and which are prevented from entering our etheric aura by insulating substances, such as rubber and silk, to mention only two. But in the work we are going to do this does not concern us and you should dismiss the matter from your mind during the present exercises.

Picture this earth contact as a swirling sphere of multicoloured light, and "feel" it as a radiant centre of heat. Practise until you can feel this "heat" very clearly. Persevere with the formulation of this centre until it is as well established as the corresponding one above the head. When this has been done, you are ready for the next part of the work.

Although you are now engaged in building up certain mental images and linking them up with the existing centres in the etheric body, you must realize that these centres are already working and that what you are doing is to establish certain mental "control machinery" in the aura in such a way that you may be able to vary the activity of these terminal points in any way you wish. Here I must warn you not to attempt any other regulation of the psychic energies involved; keep to the one I am now describing to you.

The action of the etheric energies in the physical body is known in esoteric teaching as the "burning of the fires of the body". Each particular part of the body has its own type of "fire", and there is an automatic regulation of these fires which is constantly at work. These energies, co-ordinated and working through the etheric or vital body, constitute part of what medical science terms the *vis medicatrix natura*, and their balanced action results in true physical health. Later in your instruction you will be taught more about this angle of your work; you will bear in mind that it is just as important to establish a sound inner organism, for though, as the poet says quite truly, "For of the soul the body form doth take, for soul is form, and doth the body make" it is equally true that unless the instrument (the form) which the soul is using on the physical plane is healthy, there will be distortion and misdirection of the inner forces, and this accounts for much of the vague and indeterminate illness which is found among the members of some esoteric schools. In our school we are inclined to the Roman maxim: a sound mind in a sound body, as being an ideal towards which we must work. There are exceptions, but they usually prove the general rule to be correct. There is an interaction between the two aspects of man's nature and this has been recognized in the increasing stress laid by the medical profession on what they call psycho-somatic treatment.

Any tampering with the normal action of the body fires is both foolish and dangerous, and this for two reasons. The centres of psychic energy in the inner body are located *over* certain nerve centres and glands in the physical body, and any undue concentration on, or disturbance of, these nerves and glands can badly upset the balance of the body and result in definite physical disease. Secondly, the intensification of the "fires" can result in the breaking down of a certain protective surface of the vital body, and this can cause a very great deal of trouble, both physical and super-physical.

In the lodge you will be taught how to deal with these things, and the basic laws which govern this safe approach I shall give you in the next set of instructions. For the moment I want to deal with the establishment of the two terminal points of contact, the one which brings down the solar energies, and the one which draws up the earth forces. I have used the terms "bring down" and "draw up" but actually these forces are always pressing in upon you. *What you have to do is to reduce the resistance of your personality to them.* We are usually so cluttered up with repressions and rigid thought complexes that the energies are choked back and cannot flow freely through our nature. In this exercise you are using your own conscious will to open the way for these forces to flow through you, and by this very action they will tend to restore the true balance of the bodily forces and so bring about a healthy condition both of body and mind. When someone who claims to know and practise these things is always ailing in some way or other, then you may be sure that, as *a general rule*, it is due to the wrong application of these exercises. There are certain exceptions, but these simply prove the rule. As far as you are concerned, you will find that the methods I give you will produce the desired results with the least possible trouble. I have said this last very deliberately, for at the beginning of your work on this exercise you will probably find that the effect of the conscious attempt to bring through these dynamic energies will be to cause some manifestation of bodily discomfort, even apparent disease. This, however is due to the stir-up of the various "locked-up" energies in the mind and the body. Once the circuit of force has been established, these vague but annoying symptoms will disappear and you will find that you have gained a wonderful vitality which will begin to affect the whole personality.

Sometimes this new energy, which tends to follow whatever mental path has been strongly established in the mind, can cause some annoyance, as it may well affect and stimulate certain bodily activities which we may be trying to curb. This, of course, applies most strongly to those activities which express the primal urges of self-preservation: sex and herd. The remedy is to build up new channels and the incoming forces will just as readily flow in the new river bed as in the old one. What you must not do is to worry at this stage if you find that the increased vitality is affecting you in this way.

It is because of this tendency that some teachers warn you off these exercises, but we in this school are of the opinion that with due care these things can be adjusted and controlled and need not cause undue trouble.

In the next instructions I shall send you, I will show you how to open up these energies and draw them into yourself, and at the same time I will give you the necessary safeguards against their possible misdirection.

# CHAPTER XII

## BRINGING THROUGH THE POWER

IN the last set of instructions, I gave you the method of building up the two great terminal points through which you are to draw the energies which are required for the work. Now I want to go a stage further and show you how to bring through these forces into your etheric or vital body, from which they will work upon all levels of your personality. It is important that you should remember that these forces are to be brought into the etheric, not the physical body. Since each cell in your physical body is a living thing, it possesses consciousness, of an exceedingly rudimentary type, but nevertheless consciousness, and the consciousness aspect of these millions of living cells is located in the etheric body. Thus, by charging the etheric with the energies you draw through, you affect these cells directly.

The actual psychic centres are located in the region of the spinal column, but they extend out to the surface of the etheric body; about three inches beyond the physical body itself. For the work you have to do in this preparatory training, it is important that you obey this instruction most carefully. *Never try to concentrate on the centres in the spinal column.* There are powers and forces which lie dormant therein and these, if aroused prematurely, can produce very undesirable results. This, as far as I am concerned, is not a matter of theory. So always remember this, in all your work with these powers.

There are certain perfectly safe methods of operating upon the centres. These methods use certain symbolic images as points of contact, and these symbols are taught to you at a later stage of your work. But for the present, do just as you are told, as far as the centres are concerned.

You will remember that I told you of other contact points through which the living energies must be directed, *Daath, Tiphareth,* and *Yesod.* Again, remember that it is to the surface points in the aura that your attention should be directed, and not to the actual centres within. On the Tree of Life, the *Sephiroth* corresponding to the psychic centres are shown in colour, but for the first steps in this exercise, it may be easier for you simply to visualize plain circles of white light on the surface of the etheric body. The *Sephirah Daath* is located over the throat, *Tiphareth* is over the general area of the solar and cardiac plexi, and *Yesod* over the region of the generative organs.

I want you to study these instructions very carefully, since every part of them has its reason for being there, and its omission would cause the exercise to lose much of its value.

First of all, let us consider the posture you should adopt. It is immaterial whether you lie flat upon the back, sit on your chair in the way you have already been shown, or stand erect. For preference, I would choose sitting in the god-form position, but you must find which of the three positions seems best for you. Actually, I have known people who found that the kneeling position was best for them. In these matters there is often a good deal of latitude; if the principle underlying the exercise is being properly carried out, then the position is a secondary thing. It is well to remember, however, when at a later date you perform some of the advanced exercises, you will have to adopt the postures which go with them, and not vary therefrom. For the present, however, find which position suits you best, and having done this, keep to it throughout your training.

You must now begin to use a simple breathing exercise. For the time being, forget anything which you may have read about *prana* and its connection with breathing. It is quite true that by using the breathing in a certain way, you can greatly increase your intake of this form of vital energy, but that is not the purpose of this present instruction.

You have, by visualization, built up your two terminal points, the one above your head and the other beneath your feet. The more clearly they have been built, the more effective will be your exercise. This is where so many apprentices are found out! The Magical Diary may be "faked", and for quite a time they can get by with it, but when the later exercises are attempted, they find they are unable to carry them out successfully. However, as I know from other sources that you have worked hard on these elementary exercises, I am sure that you will be able to carry out this one with complete success.

Sitting, standing, lying, or kneeling in your chosen posture, visualize the terminal centre above your head as a glowing globe or sphere of pure white brilliance. Visualize this brilliance as being so intense that its radiance streams out around it, interpenetrating your entire body. For a short time rest, as it were, in the white light, bathe in it and allow it to enter your entirely relaxed body. Then concentrate your attention upon the centre of this radiant sphere and mentally draw from it a stream of concentrated white light, at the same time taking a deep breath. Although you are breathing through the nose and inhaling the physical air, you must also see and feel yourself to be drawing in this stream of radiant energy from the very centre of the sphere of light above your head. This stream of white light should be seen mentally as being, for the moment, stored around the solar plexus centre (*Tiphareth* on the Tree of Life). You are now left with two things: a charge of air in the lungs and a charge of energy around the solar plexus. As you exhale the air from your lungs you must, at the same time, visually project the indrawn energy in the form of a shaft of light, downwards through the *Yesod* centre to merge finally into the swirling sphere of colour beneath the feet. You may notice at this point that I have made no mention of the centre above the throat, which we attribute to the *Sephirah Daath*. This for a very good reason. *Daath* is a terminal point for a very different set of energies which are coming in from another dimension, and, for the time being we are not concerned with them. Later we shall bring *Daath* into the picture.

Now comes the second part of this exercise. The charge of power which you have stored and have projected downwards to the earth centre, must now be replaced by a corresponding charge which is drawn from the earth contact beneath the feet. So, as you visualize the multi-coloured earth centre below the feet, breathe in again and visualize the energy as a shaft of orange-coloured light being drawn up through the *Yesod* and *Tiphareth* centres, into the centre above the head. Now exhale the breath, and on the next inhalation again draw upon the white brilliance. This completes the first exercise, and at the start of your practice you should complete the sequence not more than six times. It may be that you will find six times to be too many. If so reduce to half that number until you feel able to increase to the maximum. Here, as in all these things, individuals vary, and it is difficult to lay down any fixed rule. You must find out for yourself the best procedure to adopt in your own particular case. One thing, however, is definite and final; you *must not* supplement these exercises with snippets taken from Arthur Avalon's *Serpent Power* or similar works. If you break this rule then all further instruction from me will cease, and you will be held to have failed in your apprenticeship. The matter is as serious as that. I know the fascination of "Bluebeard's Chamber" can be very great (I went through this myself) but it is not simply a matter of doing something which is not in the book of rules. These energies are powerful for good or ill, and if you attempt to mix the exercises given you, with others belonging to a different system of training, then you will disorganize the finer forces in your own self, and the results of this disorganization are not good, either physically or psychically. Again, this is not a pious repetition of what someone else has written, it is something which I know from my own observation to be true. So I hope you will see the reason for this strict adherence to instructions, for therein lies safety. In any case, you will find that these exercises provide you with quite enough to do, without any additions.

When you have thoroughly established this first exercise, you will be ready to begin the second one, and this again starts from the radiant centre above the head.

When you have assumed your usual position for these exercises you can begin to visualize the radiant centre above the head, but this time you must see it as radiating a sheet of light which is the full width of your body. I have found that the best way to do this is to visualize the centre of radiance as a point in a "waterfall of light", as though you looked up at the top of a waterfall and saw the sun cutting the line at the top of the fall at its middle.

Now picture the falling sheet of light as coming down in front of you, and see it pouring around your feet. Then, quickly turn it below them *through* the earth centre and bring it back behind your body, up over your shoulders and neck, back to the centre above the head. As you do this visualization, you should breath as follows: breathe in as you first visualize the Crown Centre, then, as you exhale, visualize the sheet of light falling in front of you. As you again inhale, see the light rising behind you as I have explained. When it has been drawn back to the Crown Centre breathe out, and then, with the new inhalation, steady your attention again on that centre. This completes the cycle of operations. The complete exercise should be repeated several times, but in the beginning I would advise you to make the number the same as in the first exercise. The next exercise is similar to the first one, but the sheet of light is sent over the left shoulder, down the left side, under the feet and through the earth centre, thence back up the right side to the Crown Centre. Breathe in as you contact the Crown Centre, exhale as the light is projected down the left side; again inhale as it is brought up the right side, and, as it is poured back into the Crown Centre, you should breathe out. The number of times this should be done is the same as for the first exercise.

You are now ready for the final exercise. The consists of drawing the white radiance from the Crown Centre and mentally winding it round your body in broad wrappings of light, as though you were wrapping an Egyptian mummy in its linen bandages. Wind from the right hand side round your body to the left, and then across from the left hand side to the right. Repeat this until you have reached the feet, then continue in the same direction, but let your wrapping of light rise up the body until it is ended above the head. Inhale as you make the initial contact with the Crown Centre, exhale as you go down the body; inhale as you come back upwards and when once more you reach the Crown Centre, exhale. Again do not repeat this sequence beyond the limits of the other exercises.

So far, you have, as it were, been pulling out the energy of the radiant centre above the head. But this is only a beginning, a laying of a rough channel through which that energy may pour. Now you have to open the sluice-gates and allow the energy to pour out through you at a much higher pressure. Here you will need to use your discretion. Always remember that these forces, though divine in their origin and nature, like every other force in this manifested universe, are capable of being misused. To return to our engineering analogy, do not open the sluice-gates to more power than you can safely control.

The amount of energy which you can draw from the radiant centre is measured by your realization of it. If you think of that centre as a positive pole of the cosmic battery then you will see that it is necessary for you to have some means of checking its tremendous energy. This is equally true of the fiery centre below the feet. Here is the key to the control of the incoming energy. You have been studying and meditating on the glyph of the Tree of Life, and you will have noticed that it is said that there is a Tree in every *Sephirah*.

Our waking consciousness is centred down here in the *Kingdom*—Malkuth, and in most cases in *Malkuth* in *Assiah*. That is to say, we normally identify ourselves with the kingdom of earth in its densest and most restrictive aspect.

You must learn to centre your consciousness, for the duration of the exercise, in *Yesod* of *Malkuth*; that is, you must use the invoking formula in a carefully restricted manner. There are several forms of the invoking words, and you can choose which you will employ. I use the following: "The Fullness of Power, of Love and Wisdom pour down through me." This is the basic form. Now, according to the level of that energy which you desire to contact will be the controlling idea which you must use.

In your case you desire to work in *Yesod* of *Malkuth*, so your invocation should be somewhat as follows: "Infinite Power, Love, and Wisdom, present in all things, descend now through the most holy Gabriel and dispose and correct the designing of the representations which I have made."

Now, as you visualize the radiant centre, picture it as not only a sphere of radiance, but as a source of intense energy, powerful, pressing down into the channels you have built; a *positive*, not a negative thing.

Similarly, allow yourself to picture the earth centre in the same way, as a dynamic source of energy. If you have performed the invocation correctly, i.e., sincerely, then you will not be in danger of allowing too much of the cosmic energy to sweep through the channels you have made; you will find there is an automatic regulation in action.

I know there are those who would say, "You cannot have too much of the Divine Power; it is all good." To this the answer is that it is quite easy to have too much of a good thing, as the dying King Arthur tells Sir Bedivere in Tennyson's "Idylls of the King". By the way, this is a poem which is worth reading if you are fond of poetry. In spite of its very Victorian style, it manages to convey much of the *Morte d'Arthur* of Malory. The whole Arthurian story is the cover for a very wonderful teaching concealed within its allegory and symbolism. Try reading the Idylls or the *Morte* microcosmically, i.e., let the principal characters represent the principal parts of your own self, your ego, your psychological "shadow", etc. You may find it very interesting and helpful.

But to return to the invocation of energy. If you control the input of the cosmic life into the channels you have built, then it will work gently, but powerfully upon the various aspects of your being; and if, as is usually the case, it dissolves some of the mental complexes in your personal unconscious, the liberated energy will not surge up into consciousness in an uncontrollable flood, but it will be assimilated into your psychic economy in such a way as to strengthen rather than to overwhelm.

During many years of work and study along these lines, I have seen many who, either through ignorance or presumption, attempted to call down the cosmic life in an uncontrolled manner, and I have seen something of the trouble, and in some cases the disaster, which followed upon such ill-advised efforts.

I want you to study very carefully the whole of this instruction on the control and circulation of the cosmic energy. *Remember always, that you are working at this stage in Yesod of Malkuth, in the World of Assiah.* You are drawing in that primal power through the rainbow aura of the etheric aspect of this physical world. This should prevent you from assuming that you are far advanced. The sensations of power and the clarity of perception which result from contact with the inflowing life-power tend to make you feel that you are greater than you really are, and this can breed that pride of the false ego which leads to trouble.

# CHAPTER XIII

## "WOVEN PACES AND WAVING HANDS"

THE instructions I am sending to-day contain some of the elementary teachings about ritual and ceremonial. All being well you will become a member of a lodge engaged in ritual work; it is well, therefore, that you acquire a clear idea of its nature and use. The general distinction between ritual and ceremonial is that a "rite" is something done, while a "ceremony" is the *way in which that something is done*, but in general usage, the two terms are usually employed together.

As I daresay you know, there is considerable prejudice against ritual and ceremonial among spiritualists and the outer fringe of the psychic movement generally, and one of the favourite gambits of the average speaker on the spiritualist platforms is to refer contemptuously to the use of "dogmas, creeds, and rituals of the Christian Church" which are singled out for this attack, while strange customs from eastern sources are often taken as "the ways in which our Oriental brothers work", as I heard a speaker remark on one occasion.

There is a very definite reason for this aversion to ceremonial, on the part of the protagonists of spiritualism, and it is very largely a psychological one based upon certain subjective factors. Broadly speaking there are those who have an inherent temperamental liking for colourful ceremonial, and they will naturally gravitate to movements where such ceremonial is employed. There are also others to whom ceremonial, in its more ornate forms, is repellent. We can therefore say that there are two extreme types, ceremonialists and non-ceremonialists, with varying degrees between them. This is the basic idea which you must keep in mind.

Now, most of those who enter the psychic movements, either know nothing about ceremonial, or are in revolt against the formal orthodox Christian use of such ceremonial. Usually, the revolt against certain Christian teachings extends to the methods of worship used by them, and the catalogue of rites and ceremonies is widened to include "creeds and dogmas". As this kind of thinking is illogical, I want to write about it for a while, since I want you to be able to approach this very important part of your work without any subconscious prejudices against it, or any illogical preferences for it.

First of all, let us have a look at the word "creed". It comes, as you will know, from the Latin *credo*: "I believe", and a creed is therefore a statement of the beliefs held by a person or group of persons. Every movement, religious or secular, rests upon definite beliefs which are held by its members, and these constitute its "creed".

Now for "dogmas". If you state your belief in certain things in a definite and positive manner, then you are enunciating a dogma, for this is a term which simply means that, on the basis of what you believe, you put forward certain positive statements.

"Ritual and ceremonial" are, as I have already said, things done in a certain way. Divorced from the purely religious setting, the whole of our lives provide a perfect example of ritual work. We do things in a particular way, and we use other things to achieve this "ritual". The dining-table is laid in a familiar ritual manner, knives, forks, and spoons in customary order; an order which enables the ritual of the meal to be carried out in the best possible way. At the office, or in the workshop, we tend to evolve a certain routine which enables us to do our work with the minimum of effort and the maximum of efficiency. In the case of the workshop, we often find a ritual of work imposed upon us by the "time and motion" men. So it goes on; our whole lives are a constant rite and ceremony.

Even those who are most opposed to ritual observance in religion, the Quakers, have a ritual of "centeringdown" in the silent meeting, and by their avoidance of ritual, establish a "ritual of not being ritual".

In the case of the psychic movements and especially in the spiritualist churches, they habitually use a rather truncated version of the mass of the catechumens. This is the first part of the Christian Eucharist, and in the early days, was the only part of the service which the unbaptized and the catechumens (those under instruction) were allowed to attend. With its prayers converted into extemporary utterances by the minister, it became the form of worship of the nonconformist churches, and the early spiritualists, who were mostly rebels from the non-conformists, adapted it for their own use.

Curiously enough, the real power and function of ritual has very rarely been realized by the members of the psychic movements. I say "curiously enough" because they are the very people who should have been able to see the underlying reasons for its use, since they claim to develop and use the psychic faculties. It is in the psychological and psychic realms that the power and appeal of ritual and ceremonial is to be found.

The usual objections to the use of ritual and ceremonial are very largely based on prejudice, and are one of the legacies of the Reformation. They are identified with the practices of the Roman Catholic church, and are therefore condemned out of hand. You would find, if you question members of the various protestant bodies, that very few of the laity have anything but the vaguest idea of what the Roman church actually does, or why she does it. This is unfortunate for many reasons, one of them being the difficulty of having any rational discussion on the subject. The Orthodox eastern church is seldom considered, being vaguely thought of as some kind of variant of the Roman church.

Incense and vestments are two other things which arouse this irrational reaction. The same people, however, who object to the use of incense in the Christian church will cheerfully burn an "Oriental" joss-stick, of doubtful origin, in their seance room or private sanctuary.

As for vestments they are worth a little careful consideration since, if you enter the lodge, you will yourself be wearing the ceremonial robes of your grade. In the early days of the Christian church the ministers used to wear the "Sunday-go-to-meeting" dress of the time; this for safety reasons also, in the days of persecution. As time went on fashions changed, but the church kept the now old-fashioned dress for its ministers, and the inevitable tendency towards symbolic ornamentation began to make itself felt. So, through the centuries, the Eucharistic vestments were evolved.

If you have had any contact with the psychic healing work carried on in the spiritualistic churches, you may have noted the white coats worn by the healers. This, of course, began as an imitation of the coats worn by the medical profession in hospitals. Such coats, properly sterilized, are an aid to the general antiseptic precautions taken in these places, and to that extent would also be useful to the psychic healer. Many such white coats, however, are used which are distinctly neither sterilized nor white, and in practice they are used by the healers as a uniform of office. Given time, it is quite possible that we shall see the emergence of "healing vestments" in the same way as the churches' vestments developed.

Finally, I would draw your attention to one of the most anti-Roman and non-sacramental of Christian bodies—the Salvation Army. That they do great work among many thousands of people, work which the average churchman never even thinks of, is not to be denied. I do not wish you to think for a moment that I am, in any way, trying to disparage the work they are doing. At the same time, it is interesting to note that these people who disapprove wholeheartedly of the Catholic vestments, dress not only their ministers, but all their members in a special uniform, in fact a vestment!

You may think I am unduly critical in what I say about these various people, but it is sometimes useful to present the other side of the picture in order to correct the general ideas concerning the use or disuse of these things.

In themselves, they are of secondary importance, for the Eucharist can be celebrated, worship offered, and esoteric training done, without the use of any special dress.

But as very valuable helps in all these things, rites and ceremonies, vestments and incense, have their uses as you will find when you enter the lodge for training.

Now let me try to explain something of the underlying power and significance of ritual and ceremonial, as it is used in the lodges. First of all, there is the purely psychological value. Things are *done* in a certain way, and this way, is in itself, a teaching by "eye-gate". It is a well-known psychological teaching that the subconscious mind works very largely by picture images, and the various ritual processions and actions appeal to this by presenting vivid images to the mind.

The various actions of the rite which is being performed, tell a story, and tell it in the best possible way as far as the subconscious minds of those taking part are concerned. The rite is so constructed that the images which are built in the minds of the participants correspond to ancient and archetypal images in the depths of the mind, and these images, charged with power, are brought nearer to the surface of the personality and powerfully affect it. This is the main function of the ritual and the ceremonial of the magical lodges. The power is brought through into the conscious personality and works on all its levels, so that immediately or gradually, a definite change of consciousness is brought about.

In many of the lodges the robes used in the various rites are made with a cowl which can be drawn over the head, in order that the wearer may be completely hidden. This is very helpful; it prevents distraction and makes for impersonality. After all, the separate personalities are making up the whole of the magical rite, and in this team we do not try to spot the brilliant players; rather we look at the rite as a unity. In much the same way the vestments of the Catholic priest also emphasize his impersonality, for he is the officiant in a truly magical rite, and his personality, as such, should not come into the picture at all.

There is yet another reason for wearing robes when taking part in a magical rite. The very fact of assuming another dress tends to attune your mind to the spirit of the ceremony. This is by reason of the association of ideas, and as you begin to array yourself in the ceremonial dress, so your mind is drawn away from the outer mundane world and becomes sensitive to the subjective world in which you are going to work. Perhaps I can emphasize this by suggesting that you turn your mind back to your childhood days and recall when, with the aid of one or two articles of clothing you created for yourself a world of "cops and robbers" or "cowboys and Indians". The dress does help in the establishment of a certain frame of mind, and its presence, during the ceremony, acts as a persistent reminder of the task you are undertaking.

A word here about your robes. For the ordinary work of meditation, etc., and for the exercises which I have given you, it is not *necessary* to wear any particular dress, but nevertheless such a "meditation robe" is helpful. A simple, loose-fitting robe which can be easily slipped over the head is the kind of thing which is worn in the lodge. You can increase its efficiency by having a hood attached, and this can be drawn over the head when you are using the robe. It is very interesting to note how much this simple device tends to isolate you from outside things.

Now you will have to apply in your own way what I have told you here. In all these things, although there is a very definite occult discipline, much is left to what is known as the "ingenium" of the worker. Gain a good grasp of the principles involved, and then work them out in your own way. In my published books I have given you some of the principles, and, *within the limits of your discipline*, you are free to do a little experimenting. Do not be afraid to experiment; on the other hand do not take this for permission to "monkey with the buzz-saw", by altering any one of the exercises you have been given.

Quite apart from the psychological aspect of rites and ceremonies, there is a very real psychic aspect also, and I want, briefly, to explain something of this to you. You are already aware that in a magical rite we claim to build up an inner, psychic structure which will enable us to concentrate and direct the energies which we are about to draw through into the personal levels, and this is done by the "spell of woven paces and waving hands". But do not make the mistake of thinking that the performance of a rite without a definite mental "intention" will produce much in the way of results, though it may perhaps arouse an association of ideas, and bring through a trickle of power. The ritual work must always be the outer expression of a real inner purpose.

Now when you perform a ritual "with intention", as we say, you will be building up a definite set of thought images, and those of us who possess the clairvoyant faculty can see that these thought images are formed in the plastic substance of the astral light. It is these images which form the conducting channels for the inner energies which we call down into our personal sphere.

We are *building* a composite thought-form, and for this reason the terminology of the building trade is very applicable, and most of the ritual orders make use of it. You will, of course, be familiar with its use in connection with the very wonderful masonic order.

(It is true that for the greater number of its members such a thing as thought-form building is quite non-existent, but that does not alter the fact that, if they sincerely take part in the Craft ritual, they do actually build such forms.)

Here I want to give you a word of warning. That which you can build by intention and rite, can equally be broken down by a suitable use of intention and rite. It follows, then, that on all matters connected with such thought-building, it is necessary to preserve secrecy. This is the real reason for the secrecy of the lodge working. It is not that no one knows the general rituals, for they have been published openly, or semi-openly, many times. What is important is that the workings of the lodge concerned should be kept secret. Each lodge is on its own "contact" as we say, and it is the form of its ritual work which must be kept secret.

The great psychologist Jung has some rather disparaging remarks to make about occult secrecy: He points out, quite rightly, that it is possible to acquire a kind of "guilt-complex" with regard to the secret work, and to develop, in addition, a "cut-off" attitude towards those who "are not of us". This, of course, is a possibility, but if the lodge is giving true teaching, all its activities will be correlated with the everyday activities of the brethren, and then this occult secrecy is seen to be simply the equivalent of the notice on the workshop door: "Keep out, men at work."

It is, of course, well known that many secret societies have been used for political purposes, and in many cases for politically subversive purposes. In the true lodges, however, party politics of any kind have no place. All meet in equality on the floor of the lodge, and the workings of the lodge are directed towards the building and transformation of character. No attempt is made to interfere, either overtly or covertly in the political sphere. All history has shown the folly of attempting such political work. An outstanding example is the endeavour made by the Polish Chasidim to influence the Napoleonic wars in Europe.

In the group-thought-form which is built up by the use of ritual, there are certain focal points where the influences which well up from the deeper strata of the collective unconscious of the race, are brought into contact with the group, and charge the form with their own particular energy. The officers of the lodge are, to use a technical term, "contacted" on these focal points. They thus become channels through which the energies concerned enter into, and charge up, the composite thought-form.

So, behind each officer there is built up a certain figure which represents the power of his or her office. These telesmatic images are strongly visualized by the officers concerned and also by the higher-grade brethren who are present. They are part of the mechanism whereby the deeper forces of the collective unconscious are channelled into the group. You will hear them referred to as the "god-forms", and you will have to learn how to build up such forms, and, though this comes at a later stage, you will learn how to link up the forms with the forces they symbolize, and of which they will be the channels.

I only touched upon this part of the subject because I want you to see how important are your "five-finger exercises" in visualization. This may help you in those "dry" periods when the heavens are as brass, and it seems as if any proficiency you may have gained in the past has been lost.

Now I think I have given you as much as you need at this stage of your training, and I want you to meditate upon what you have been told and I *do* mean *meditate*. The implications of what I have told you are really far-reaching and steady meditation should help you to comprehend them.

In your next instructions, I will try to answer your queries in connection with some difficulties you seem to be having in your training, and we will see if any light can be thrown upon them. However, whether things go smoothly or otherwise, *persevere with the exercises.* Do not make the mistake of stopping until you hear from me. This can be a subtle way of dodging the work involved, for the subconscious levels can, and do, make use of such things.

At the same time, of course, since you are under the training of the lodge, you are also under its protection, and should things become too much for you, do not hesitate to shout for help; it will be forthcoming.

# CHAPTER XIV

# "THERE ARE LIONS IN THE WAY"

I GATHER from your report this month that you are having some difficulty in carrying out your exercises, and that this difficulty arises from within yourself and not from outer conditions. From the tone of your letter you seem to be thoroughly depressed and inclined to throw up the whole thing.

I have been expecting something like this to happen; it is one of the signs that you really have been trying to put into practice all that you have been given. Now let me explain why I have been expecting these "lions in the way", as they are sometimes described. When you first undertook training along these lines, you were full of enthusiasm and determined to do everything in your power to follow all the instructions you were given. Perhaps, like myself, in the early days of my own training, you regarded it as an exciting quest; something after the style of the adventures of King Arthur's knights of the Round Table? Actually, it is such a high adventure, but it needs to be considered in its correct perspective.

Taking the Arthurian stories at their face value (actually they are romance presentations of a much more ancient and wonderful teaching), have you ever thought of the real work involved in the making of a knight? His long apprenticeship as page and squire, his strenuous exercises in the tilt-yard with sword and lance, with spear and shield? The inevitable envy and jealousy, as well as the comradely rivalry between himself and his companions? The long, dull, and arduous chores which must be done if he was one day to ride and fight behind his own banneret? All these things, as well as the rough treatment and the many temptations to which he was subjected, must have caused much distress to the would-be knight, particularly if he was of a sensitive type. He must have gone through many periods of depression and doubt before the final vigil in the dark and empty church before the dawn of the day of his accolade.

I would counsel you to meditate on these things. Use the visualizing power which you have developed, and make these scenes live. It may seem that they are simply the representations of purely mundane conditions in a rough social environment, but they are also true parables of the conditions which your own self has to encounter. You will remember that, at the very beginning of your training, I warned you that this apprenticeship was not entirely a "bed of roses"; that you would find yourself beset by difficulties. I was obliged to give you this warning, and I was fully aware that, although in the first flush of enthusiasm, you would probably minimize them, at a later date they would cause you dismay and some distress of mind. In this I appear to have been correct, so we must now consider carefully just what are the reasons for these difficulties, how they may be surmounted, and how they may even be turned into aids and opportunities for advancement.

In what I have written about the knightly preparation I have tried to get you to see these things as part of the training; as the parallel bars, the box, the ropes, and all the other paraphernalia of the gymnasium; for this is what they really are, the tools whereby you may reshape your personality in accordance with the teaching you are receiving.

This personality is to become a well-tempered and efficient tool in the hands of your own true Self, and you have the task of shaping and tempering it accordingly. You will notice that I have written "Self" with the capital letter. This is because I want you to realize that the "self" with which you usually identify yourself, is not the real centre of your being; though you may centre all your personal desires and thoughts around it, making yourself "self-centred". The true centre of your being is that higher aspect of your nature about which you have learnt, and around which it will become necessary at a certain stage for you to re-centre the whole of your personality in order that you may become "SELF-centred".

All the training which you will receive in the lodge will be directed towards this achievement, for it is very true that only by the entire surrender of the personal will to that higher Self, can you become an efficient knight in the spiritual legions.

"The King will follow Christ, and we the King", say the knights in Tennyson's poem, and this is also the sequence in the inner kingdoms. For the higher Self always follows the indwelling Christ, and the personal self must learn to follow its inner King.

I daresay you will be thinking that this is a lot of pious and mystical advice which does not seem to you to be very helpful. This was my own reaction in the early days of my apprenticeship, but nevertheless what I have said is the necessary groundwork for that with which I desire to impress you now. You are under training for the lodge, and the most important part of that training consists of being taught how to serve others. For in the lodges we work as a team, and the team spirit must be cultivated by all who take part in the rites. Everything

depends upon the development of this team spirit, for it builds up
what is known as a "group-mind" and it is by the use of this group-
mind that the inner forces are directed and controlled. You will see,
therefore, how essential it is for you to learn in a team. In a team there
is little use for selfish individual brilliance; the talents of all the participants must be subordinated to the work as a whole, and it is this
subordination of the personal self which many aspirants find so very
difficult. However, if you are to do any real work in the lodge, it is
absolutely essential that you develop this power of sinking yourself
into the team. Just as the team spirit in a football team does not mean
that the individuals who make up the team play less well when playing together than they do when practising their own particular
methods by themselves, so it is in magical work. You will find as you
proceed with your training, that there are certain aspects in which
you feel more at home than in others, and there is no reason why you
should not specialize along these lines at a later stage. However, just
as the squire had to learn not only the use of the sword, but also of
the spear, lance, and shield, so it is also necessary that you should
learn to do these things efficiently; these things which you now find
difficult and less congenial.

All this, of course, means that your own little personal self is going
to suffer a good many shocks and will naturally try to assert its own
point of view. It does this as a rule, by generating emotions which
indicate to the seeing eye exactly where the shoe pinches! The most
usual of these emotional outbursts is jealousy, an emotion which you
can very usefully dispense with at any stage of your life, quite apart
from matters esoteric.

If you should find yourself becoming jealous of anyone, then be
sure that this is a silly and irrational impulse from your own personal
self, the "false ego" as it is termed by the psychologists. It often
happens that such a reaction to the work *in the lodge* is transferred to
*people outside its doors* and many beginners go on proudly thinking
that they have obeyed instructions and have overcome the fault. This
of course, is only one of the ways in which the false ego attempts to
get away with it. This is very much of a lion in the way and has to be
watched for and overcome. If you find that you are being jealous of
someone at your work or in your home, or circle of acquaintances,
then take steps at once to eliminate it.

I say "eliminate" it, but just as there is always a characteristic vice
to every virtue, so there is a virtue to every vice. If you tackle this
jealousy in the correct way, you will not try to eliminate it by a direct
frontal attack, but will follow the occult method of balancing up the

unbalanced force, which this vice of jealousy really is, and so turning it into a positive virtue.

The very fact that you are jealous of someone, means that you are at least aware of certain standards which are desirable. Of course, you will have identified these standards with *your* ideas and actions, but at least you have realized that it is possible for people to have certain standards and individual skills. Now you have to redirect your ideas into more positive and impersonal channels. By "impersonal" I do not mean a cold appraisal of the work, but rather an attitude of keen enthusiasm for it in itself, irrespective of your own part therein. Also, though fully and happily conscious of the way your own contribution fits into the overall picture, you will be looking all the time for opportunities to help your brethren in their part of the work, even as they will also be keen to assist you in yours. If you will maintain this attitude of mind consistently over a period of time, you will find it to be an excellent corrective to any jealousy you may have developed. The same technique will work in all similar cases.

The troubles you mention are not very serious, and since you have been carrying out faithfully the instructions I have given you, there is no particular danger. The difficulties you mention are well-known and are incidental to the stage of training through which you are now passing. There are, however, two other lions which you may meet in the way. The first is "time and tide". You will remember that in the Bible it is said that there is a time for all things: "a time for marriage, and a time for giving in marriage; a time for sowing and a time for reaping; a time for speech and a time for silence." This is very true, but when we first start on this training we are sometimes forgetful of this law of rhythmic return, and it often happens that the apprentice tries vigorously to work against the prevailing tide rather than with it.

Here you see the need for the exercise of the virtue of discrimination: you must follow the tides of your own inner being, but at the same time watch that you are not allowing this to become an excuse for laziness!

There are four great tides which will affect you, even as they affect all life on this planet. In your case, however, since you are beginning to tread the path, the effects of these tides will be more apparent than in the case of an ordinary person. I mentioned the tides in one of my books, but I will just go over them again in order to refresh your memory.

The first tide is that which commences with the Winter Solstice, around December 21st, and continues until the Vernal Equinox in

March. This is known as the "Tide of Destruction" and its characteristic *is* destruction. Not destruction in the total sense of the word,
but the destruction of anything which is effete or ill-balanced in life.
So during this period, expect that all those plans for the future, which
you have formulated, will be thoroughly tested and tried by the
winds of adversity. Anything which is not built upon the rock will be
overthrown. This, of course, is a very helpful thing, for it enables us
to clear away much of the flotsam and jetsam which we have accumulated, and much of which we have built into the very fabric of our
being. The next tide begins at the Vernal Equinox and continues until
the Summer Solstice in June. This is the "Tide of Planting and Sowing": the time when you should plant and sow those ideas and ideals
which have survived the Tides of Destruction. Then comes the "Tide
of Reaping" from the Summer Solstice until the Autumnal Equinox
in September: during the flow of which the harvest of these ideas and
ideals will be reaped. This harvest is of many kinds; it is gathered on
many planes of life and consciousness, and in order that it may be
truly gathered in, *it is essential that it be reaped here in the physical
world also*. Anyone who attempts to go forward, without taking this
into account, will rue it.

The last tide is the "Tide of Formulation", which continues until
the Winter Solstice. This tide is the one in which you may form your
plans for the future, examine your past successes and failures, and
evaluate your general progress. It is well for you to remember that in
the true sense, progress can be made through what may seem to you
to be utter failure. As a matter of fact, the only real failure is to stop
trying. As long as you get up again after each fall, you are doing well.

All four tides, of course, merge one into the other, and there is no
sharp dividing line between them, so you can expect their mixed influences to affect you at the end of one tide and the beginning of the
next. I will leave you to work out for yourself what times and seasons
are best for any particular type of esoteric work. Remember, however, that ultimately you must be able to swim against the tides, and
even to use their energy in the same way that a boat "tacks into the
wind", and so sails against it.

There remains the second lion, which we term "The Dark Night of
the Soul". It is more commonly found in those who follow the mystic
path, but it also affects those who follow the occult line of work. It is
an intense depression of spirits, a feeling of utter failure and un-
worthiness. Part of this effect is due to the inescapable contrast between the ecstacies and delights of contact with the inner worlds, and
the darkness of this mundane plane. The other part is due to nervous

overstrain. Again, the remedy is to cut down immediately on the formative side of your work and lengthen your periods of relaxation. Hold on, and the natural tides will swing you clear of the "Slough of Despond".

You will remember that Pilgrim in the *Pilgrim's Progress*, fell into this slough of despond *after* he had set out on the heavenly journey. Do not expect to be shielded from these things just because you have started out on the esoteric path.

As I have already said, meditate on these things, and particularly try to cultivate that first virtue of the path. You can get through; others have.

# CHAPTER XV

## "THE GATES ARE OPEN"

IT is now some time since you wrote to me complaining of the spiritual "dryness" you were experiencing, and I have noted with pleasure that you appear to have passed the test quite well. As your records show, there has been real progress. It often happens that this Dark Night of the Soul comes just before a very critical point in the training of the apprentice. This was so in your own case, for I am happy to tell you now that the artificer under whom we work has intimated that you have now reached the point in your training when you are eligible for admission to the lodge, should this be your wish. I must not attempt to influence you in any way in the making of your decision, though I am in duty bound to give you a brief idea of all that lies before you should you take this step.

In the training which you have received from me, you have not only been given a philosophy of life, but you have been taught some of the practical work which you will have to do when you enter the Mysteries. Besides this you have been "contacted", or linked with, certain inner forces, and these forces have been moulding you along certain very definite lines, so that real growth has taken place in your psychic and spiritual make-up.

You have now to adapt and adjust the unfolding life-pattern which is yours so that it fits not only into the plan of your own deeper self, but also into the pattern of the lodge wherein you will work. For, never forget, the basis of the lodge work is *group* working, not solitary endeavour, though this latter is, of course, a very necessary addition to the teamwork of the group. In any case, membership of a group does help you to "see yourself" as you are, enabling you at the same time to see where you are going wrong by comparing your results with those obtained by your brethren in the lodge, enabling, also, those who rule therein to correct any errors in your work.

In the lodge you will be working as a member of a closely knit team, and the rituals in which you will take part will integrate you into the "group mind" of the fraternity. This group work is very important, though, in addition, much personal work will be required of you. The momentum of the group-mind will often swing you over the periods of "dryness" and enable you to maintain your contact with the inner forces. At the same time, however, you must learn to stand alone without that support. It is this very combination of teamwork and individual effort which is such an important part of esoteric training.

You will find that there is a very real discipline in the lodge, and under that discipline you must work. There is no question here of attempting to vary that discipline by popular vote. But always remember that you must be obedient to the discipline of your order, and that it is to the rule of the order, and not to its officers, that you are asked to give allegiance.

In chapter, in your lodge, you will have the opportunity of putting forward any query or complaint you may have; without inviting any future reprisals. But at the same time, if you harbour any suppressed thoughts of envy or distrust, you will find yourself being slowly, but very effectively, extruded from the group-mind, and you will eventually leave. But just as such a thought, strongly held in the mind, can extrude you from the brotherhood, so a thought of aspiration can be supported by the group mind, and that support will enable you to contact levels of consciousness which you, at your present stage, would not be able to reach.

Now I want to give you some idea of what you will be doing in your lodge, should you decide to enter it. To do this, I must give you the general picture of the work of the esoteric orders. First of all, I must warn you against supposing that the lodges indulge in the somewhat lurid antics which many writers of occult fiction portray in their books. Of course there *are* many small groups which do specialize in the more spectacular side of the esoteric work, but as a general rule the lodge work is rather hum-drum until you begin to get below the surface appearances and see the real work which is being performed, and also realize something of the mighty power of the unseen forces with which the lodge is dealing.

Now, as briefly as I can, I want to give you a picture of the work of the fraternities. What I am going to tell you, cannot be proven by you at present, and it might be that you could work in the lodge for many years before any such proof was available, and for the present, at least, you will have to take what I am going to say on trust.

There exists a mighty Spiritual Council which, beyond the veils of earthly time and space, is the real government of this planet. Its members are those "spirits made perfect" who are hinted at in all the world-scriptures, and who are incorporated in a great hierarchy ranging from mighty flaming intelligences: "Spirits before the Throne", "Watchers and Holy Ones", down through many grades of being, to the ordinary men and women who work in their service. Indeed the chain extends even further, into that realm where the elemental spirits are struggling into material manifestation.

In the properly constituted lodge of the Mysteries, all these grades are represented, even the Mighty Ones who are invoked and who respond to the invocation, and are manifest in the "presence-form" on the inner planes.

It is into this living chain of light that you are introduced when you are initiated into the lodge, and you will see why those of us, who have been so privileged, are so insistent upon the worthiness of those whom we attempt to recruit into the service of the light. What then, is required of you, when you stand blind-fold before the portals of the Mysteries? Prompted by your guide, you will knock thrice upon that door, and one who is within will ask you "Who knocks?" You will reply: "One who desires to enter your lodge and learn from your teachers." Then the voice will ask the crucial question, "Why do you desire to enter our lodge and to learn from our teachers?" To this question there is only one answer, an answer which your guide will prompt you to give, "I desire to know in order to serve." This, which you will say with your mouth, you must also affirm with your heart, and there must be no duplicity, else will the initiation fail, and although you may enter the lodge, yet will you be cut off from your brethren, and in due course will find yourself being extruded from the brotherhood, even as Nature works to eliminate a foreign body from any living organism. Think carefully over this, for it is better to turn away from the temple door than to enter with a falsehood on your lips.

If you decide to go forward into the lodge you must be prepared to accept its discipline. You may feel that, since you have already received a good deal of teaching and have also developed some proficiency in the basic magical work, you are entitled to skip the elementary training in the lodge. If you think this, then you will be mistaken. The object of the elementary training in the lodge is not only to give the brethren certain factual teaching, but also, and this is most important, to integrate the neophyte into the group mind of the fraternity.

For this reason, in all reputable lodges of the Mysteries, this basic work is insisted on, no matter what knowledge or previous experience the newcomer may have. In fact, if he does possess such knowledge, he is subjected to the discipline with especial thoroughness. This was certainly so in my case, and I realized at a later date, that this had been for my own good, as well as for the general welfare of the lodge.

I would counsel you, therefore, not to be discouraged if you find the early training somewhat irksome. Remember, you are not only being instructed and integrated into the group-mind of your fraternity; you are also being trained in character, in order that you may take your place in the ranks of the servers of light; you must "serve your time" as a hewer of wood and a drawer of water for your brethren, as well as taking your turn as doorkeeper in the temple, before you can hope to sit between the pillars on the Throne of the East.

In your lodge you will find that there are certain grades through which you must pass, and each grade has its own discipline and methods. But all lead to an active participation in the work of the fraternity. The fraternity works as the pendant of an invisible Order, and all its work is designed so to assist you in the great work of the regeneration of your own self, that you may be a craftsman and take your place in the ranks of light. If all the resources of the lodge are available to you in accordance with your grade, so all the powers and skills which you may develop must be freely offered by you for service.

Remember this in the heat and burden of the day, and remember it too when the way seems dull and uninteresting.

When you enter your lodge as a neophyte, you will be asked to take a certain oath, and in some lodges the neophyte is shown this oath before he enters, in order that he may see that he will be called upon to do only those things which are in line with the true moral law. He will not be required to go beyond this at any point in his esoteric work, nor will he be required to give unqualified obedience to any person in the lodge, for obedience is to the rule of the fraternity; and all, from "those who rule in the lodge" down to the latest joined apprentice, are bound by the rule. Always remember this.

Above all, as I have already said, do not expect to find yourself in the spectacular glamorous lodge so vividly portrayed by many writers of occult fiction. Indeed, should you ever find yourself in such surroundings, it would be a signal for you to get out as quickly as you could.

What you will find, in the lodge into which you are being admitted, is a well-ordered ritual, simple yet dignified, and a teaching which will answer many questions, together with a training which will yield results. Those results are, of course, contingent upon the perseverance and energy which you bring to the task, but I can assure you from personal experience that this is a path which, if you follow it with perseverance, discrimination, and energy, will bring you, as it has brought many others, into the light.

Beyond lie many grades and levels of achievement in what are termed the Greater Mysteries, but these heights will only be trodden by you when you have, to some extent at least, slain the kings of unbalanced force in your own nature. The rough ashlar, the crude and unshapen mass of your present personality must be shaped into the polished cubic stone, square and true, of a truly regenerate personality.

Our next meeting will be in the lodge, where, beneath the soft radiance of the everburning flame above you, and with the light upon the altar casting its wavering radiance upon the symbols thereon, you will take the Oath of the Mysteries, and I, ruling in the East, will accept that oath, and, by virtue of my office, bring you into our brotherhood.

The gates stand open; enter into light.

# MAGIC AND THE QABALAH

To

**THE REVERED MEMORIES**

of

"R.K.", "D.N.F." and "A.V.O."

# CHAPTER I

# A GENERAL INTRODUCTION

IT was Omar Khayam who lamented that he had, when young, heard great argument among the philosophers, "but evermore came out by that same door wherein I went." Very many men throughout the ages have echoed this lament. According to esoteric teachings, however, there has always existed a body of knowledge based upon the direct personal experience of men of exceptional quality. This direct experience has been explained and codified by teachers, who, from the beginning of human life on this planet, have constituted a guiding body known variously as "The Brotherhood", or the "College of the Holy Spirit".

This teaching has been checked and verified by generations of seers. It is the *Corpus Hermeticus,* a faith and a belief, limited in its expression in any particular age or period of time. The esoteric student is indeed a "spiritual scientist", and is always trying to express this basic philosophy in the forms of his own day; but because this is not only a *received philosophy* but also, primarily, a "theosophy" capable of being checked and verified by its followers, it is a living teaching, opening up new vistas of thought and action.

There are certain powers and faculties in man which enable him to verify the teachings for himself, and to make a living contact with the inner side of things; and, since humanity is *one,* it is evident that these powers are latent in all men. They are the so-called "psychic" faculties, and are variously developed in mankind. In some cases they are only a little below the surface, in others, they are buried so deeply that it is not possible to bring them to any great degree of functioning, though even this partial emergence can give a basis upon which the individual concerned may construct a helpful and workable philosophy of life.

Where they are near the surface, the psychic faculties tend to appear spontaneously, and there exists a "rule of thumb" method of bringing them into activity that has been used throughout the ages; a method quite apart from those so carefully designed and controlled in the esoteric schools.

However, even though these psychic faculties do not manifest in the waking consciousness, it should be clearly understood that they are always working below the surface, thereby influencing the deeper subconscious levels.

This is important, for in these deep unconscious levels of the mind of man, exist the great driving forces known as the instincts. We are used to their classification under the headings of "self-preservation", "sex", and the "herd" instincts. Jung has pointed out that there is yet another basic instinct in man, the religious instinct, an instinct just as powerful as any of the others. For this reason it has been found impossible to pin-point the exact time in human evolution when religious observances began. This religious instinct manifested itself in two ways. The first was a *direct* experience, by certain individuals, of an underlying reality behind the physical world, the second, a formalized theology concerning this experience. Such theology exteriorized itself in the ritual and ceremonial worship of the tribe.

Since this direct experience did not come to everyone, it tended to be withdrawn; to persist as an inner grouping behind the outer religious form. So, through the ages, all the great religions developed this two-fold aspect, and in their "Mysteries" the man who was prepared and ready, was initiated into a method of direct experience of the hidden realities.

In the early days of Christianity, the "Mysteries of Jesus" withdrew into the background, while, at the same time, the whole vast movement of Gnosticism was expelled from the church. It is true that many of the gnostic schools were aberrant in both teaching and moral conduct; but whether any real good was gained by ignoring the implication of our Lord's parable of the wheat and the tares is a debatable point. It is clear, however, that as a result of this wholesale expulsion, any manifestation of direct experience tended to be either suppressed or twisted to fit into an already existing theology. This attitude has persisted up to the present day.

In modern times this field of direct experience has, under the name of "extra-sensory-perception" (or E.S.P.), been studied from an objective and scientific point of view, and a new branch of research, entitled "parapsychology", has been started and now flourishes in many parts of the world. These powers of extra-sensory-perception, usually known as the psychic faculties, are sometimes referred to by American writers as "wild talents", and at first sight they seem to have little relevance to normal life. They emerge unexpectedly, and in many cases do not seem to be under the control of their possessor.

In Victorian days it was customary to attribute them to the unscientific observations of uneducated or primitive people, to mention unbalance, or even to simple fraud. This point of view has gradually been modified in many respects, and there now exists a group of scientifically minded people who are prepared to admit the possibility of such supernormal powers. Humanity in general, however, has not waited for their permission to go ahead in its growing belief in the existence of these powers and faculties. In the lives of the great religious teachers their followers have noted the use of such powers by both the teachers themselves and by their immediate disciples, though they usually claimed that the supernormal phenomena produced by their own particular teacher were superior to those produced by other teachers. They have even asserted that the wonders exhibited by the others were either fraudulent, or the work of evil beings attempting to deceive the faithful.

This idea was common in the early days of Christianity and it still persists in many denominations of the church. But quite apart from the specific phenomena associated with the teachers and their immediate disciples, there has always existed a belief, based on experience, that powers of this kind were possessed by people who were not of the orthodox persuasion, people who were indeed active in their opposition to it. Such supernormally gifted people became, what might be termed, a psychic "Cave of Adullam";* and to them resorted all who were in opposition to the established orthodoxy of the day.

So the "Camp of the Gifted Ones", came to include some very questionable characters: thus giving the orthodox a good excuse for persecution. But persecution only tends to strengthen any belief, and these natural psychics and seers persisted through the centuries, sometimes as solitary "wise men" and "wise women", and sometimes as members of the witch-cult, a cult which was simply the remnant of the old pre-Christian religion. With the advent of Christianity the non-Christian religions were reduced to scattered groups of worshippers in remote country places, hence the name "pagan" which was applied to them.

However, a considerable period of time was to pass before the church became seriously worried by these vestiges of the old religions, but with the growth and secularization of Christianity, it entered into a persecuting phase and began the attempt to root out these obstinate people. The two classes of the persecuted, the psychics and the pagans, found it helpful to join forces against the common enemy, and their gain in strength was such that they became a real threat to the interests of the church. Then there set in the era of persecution which constitutes such a dark page of Christian history. With the Reformation, it might have been thought that these unfortunate people would have had some respite from their troubles. The very godly reformed churches, however, here and elsewhere, continued to be just as bitter in their attempts to stamp out these heresies. A new outlook arose in the seventeenth and eighteenth centuries, and belief in supernormal powers began to wane; concurrently the persecution of witches and wizards began to lessen, though it had a sharp recurrence in the Salem witchcraft trials in the New England States in America.

* I Samuel, xxii, 1 and 2

In the nineteenth century, however, modern spiritualism, both in America and on the continent of Europe, began to revive the belief in the existence of supernormal powers, — and the extreme fringe of the new psychic movements began to link up with the surviving remnants of the witch-cult. These remnants were, as a rule, no more than a degraded expression of the old non-Christian religion. The witches had, generally speaking, reverted to the roles they had played in classical times, as fortune tellers, poisoners and abortionists. Even today, in most large towns they are still to be found telling fortunes by greasy packs of Tarot cards, casting spells with the use of "dragon's blood" and mercury, and very often acting as the means by which unfortunate girls can be put in touch with the abortionists.

Let us add that true witch-cult still flourishes free from this sordid element: it is simply a body of people who worship under the old non-Christian forms. In varying degrees it still uses the psychic abilities of those of its members who can be trained along this line, but in the main it has nothing to do with the parody which existed in the Middle Ages; a parody due to the ruthless persecution it endured.

We have, therefore, several lines of unorthodox belief all acknowledging the existence of supernormal faculties, and making use of them in varying degrees. The fortune-teller we have always with us, and the spiritualists have formed a religious cult based, in the main, upon the revelations which they have received from the "other side", whilst the Theosophical movement has brought to the western world some of the wisdom of the Orient. This has found a considerable measure of acceptance, since there has always existed a tradition that others, apart from the witches and wizards, possessed a wisdom and power hidden from the generality of mankind.

In the West, in pre-Christian times, this wisdom was thought to be in the possession of the initiated priests and leaders of what we now term the "Mystery-Religions", which sprang up in the Mediterranean lands some time before the advent of Christianity. More particularly the Egyptian and Chaldean Mystery Schools were thought to possess this hidden knowledge in its fullness, and many great philosophers of the ancient world sought initiation in their assemblies.

When, in the early Christian days, the emperor Justinian closed down the pagan philosophical schools, it was commonly thought that the hidden teachings had been finally suppressed, and this opinion has been generally held by the majority of European scholars who have considered the subject. However, an unbiassed study of the matter soon suggests that the hidden wisdom not only survived the destruction of the Roman Empire, but also that it exists today.

Side by side with the tremendous advances in scientific knowledge which are so characteristic of these modern days, there has been a parallel increase in the number of organisations which claim to possess some part of what has come to be known as the "ancient" or "ageless" wisdom. Much of what is taught in these modern schools of esoteric thought is a re-hash of certain teachings derived from the East where the indigenous Mystery-tradition has never been suppressed. Much that is being exported from the Orient is, however, but a superficial presentation of the true eastern wisdom. Not every "swami" or "rishi" is worthy of these venerable titles.

This eager acceptance of oriental teachings is characteristic of many of the modern esoteric movements; human nature being what it is (and not what we might wish it to be) the demand has created a corresponding supply. However, as the great psychologist, Jung, has pointed out in his writings, the eastern systems are unsuited to most western peoples.

There is, of course, no reason at all why the oriental philosophies should not be *studied* in conjunction with the western systems of thought, and some philosophers and theologians (mainly in the Roman Catholic Church), are doing this with profitable results. It is a matter not merely of understanding the deeper aspects of these eastern teachings, but also of following the methods of training which have been developed in connection with them. It is here that the possibility of trouble arises. These methods, usually summed up under the general title of "yoga", have been developed for oriental outlooks and requirements, and for the particular physical make-up of eastern peoples. In spite of the earnest endeavours being made at the present time to assure us that there is no difference between East and West, it remains true, at least in the field of esoteric training, that differences do exist and have to be reckoned with. There is, of course, much common ground, but yoga, to be really helpful to the *occidental* student, has to be considerably modified.

However, just as the East has its own characteristic methods of esoteric teaching and training, based upon certain sacred writings and the accumulated experiences of its trained initiates through many centuries; so in the West there is a similar method of training, adapted for the psychological and physical make-up of western peoples, based upon the Jewish and Christian Scriptures, and possessing, also, a deposit of the recorded experiences of generations of seers and students, together with the fragmentary records of wisdom derived from times long past.

This basic body of pre-historic teaching and practice has been enriched during historic times through contacts made by the Hebrew nation with the various Mystery Schools, which sprang up, as we have said, in the Mediterranean lands during the classical era. The enforced contacts of the Hebrews with other nations during the sojourns in Egypt and Assyria and, still further afield, with other elements of value, such as, for instance, the native philosophy usually associated with the Celtic Druids (*but deriving from pre-Celtic* times), all these contributed valuable material to this composite tradition of the West.

In all esoteric systems worthy of the name, much use is made of symbols and symbol-systems, and in the East, certain composite symbols, terms "mandalas", have been developed and used. So also, similar composite symbols, which are known as "glyphs" are used in the western schools of esoteric training, and the key glyph, around which all the other associated symbolism of the western training is centred, is the "mighty all-embracing glyph of the universe and the soul of man", known as *Otz Chiim,* the "Tree of Life".

The symbolism of the Tree of Life is basically derived from the esoteric teachings of the past, but has been added to in all the centuries of its existence by those who have used it as an instrument of training. For it is more than a diagram; it is the result of many centuries of training and experience gathered into pictorial form; it is also an instrument through which certain energies and forces may be contacted by successive generations of students.

This glyph comes to us down the centuries and is a part, indeed the most important part, of the system of teaching known as the Qabalah which was evolved by the Hebrew nation. This name, QBL, may be translated as "from mouth to ear", and, though written records have also been used to supplement it, the main body of esoteric knowledge has always been handed down by oral instruction.

Such written records were, and still are, kept secret, and it was not until the eleventh century of our era that any part of the secret teaching was put into print for general use. Even then, the Qabalists reserved the inner teaching and did not allow it to be given out to all and sundry.

Much of this pre-Christian teaching was carried over from Jewry in the early Christian Church, and there, mixed with Egyptian, Persian and Grecian elements, it formed the basis of the great Gnostic movement in the early days of the church. Then for various reasons, the church expelled the Gnostics from its fellowship, and threw away, at the same time, most of the keys to the inner teaching, so that the Qabalistic tradition was handed on, in the main, in purely Jewish circles; though certain Muslim teachers used it in a modified form.

With the increasing power of the church, the arcane schools became subject to varying degrees of persecution, and with the abolition by Justinian of the schools of philosophy, the tradition went into hiding, though, every now and then, fragmentary gleams of its presence shone out amid the deepening gloom of the Dark Ages in Europe.

In the tenth and eleventh centuries, some of the Qabalistic circles in Spain published, for the first time, part of their teachings, and on these, as a parallel movement, there sprang up a school of Christian Qabalism.

Unfortunately, an attempt was made to use the Qabalistic teaching as an instrument for the conversion of the Jews to the Roman Catholic faith. This caused the study of the Qabalah to be condemned by the strictly orthodox rabbis of that time, resulting in an antipathy which persisted down the years, and exists today, except perhaps, in the Liberal Synagogues of the Jewish faith.

The Qabalah has been used by several schools of thought since the days of Moses de Leon and his school, among them being an unorthodox sect of Jews known as the "Chasidim", whose chief exponents in the early nineteenth century were the "wonder-working rabbis" of Poland. Some of these men attempted to use their wonder-working powers in connection with the Napoleonic wars in Europe. A fine account of this is to be found in Martin Buber's *Sons of Heaven*. The Chasidim still exist as a sect, and are strong in certain American circles.

The Qabalah was also used by two other schools of unorthodox thought, the Alchemists and the Rosicrucians. Both these schools used it as the framework of their philosophy, and incorporated into it the esoteric tradition they had received from their predecessors. The Arabs had brought much of the learning of the Egyptian lands into Western Europe, where it was received under the name of "alchemy", a word based upon the old name for Egypt: "Khem". Thus alchemy was "the Egyptian matter": the secret teaching of Egypt.

Again, in the story of the putative founder of the Rosicrucians, Christian Rosencreutz, it is said that he journeyed to "Damcar" (probably Damascus) and later to Fez, where, it is stated, he studied "their Qabalah".

The Western esoteric tradition is generally identified with the Rosicrucian order, most of its teaching being based upon the Rosicrucian adaptation of the Qabalah, interwoven with the strands of tradition which have been handed down from both pagan and Christian gnosis.

All esoteric schools have a central symbol system, around which their teaching is organized, and the Western "mandala", as these symbol-systems are named in the orient, is, as we have said, *Otz Chiim*, the Tree of Life. In the more extravagant claims made by some of its exponents, the Qabalah is said to have been taught to Adam in Paradise, by the Archangel, Metratron, and the Tree of Life is identified as that tree which the Scriptures tell us grew in the Garden of Eden. This, of course, is only a way of saying that this particular body of teaching and practice comes from a remote antiquity, and is therefore worthy of consideration. However, claims to such ancient lineage are really beside the point (many teachings and practices that are far from edifying can also claim remote ancestry) so it is advisable to be guarded in making such claims on behalf of any system of thought, unless the objective proof can be given of such early origins.

In the world of "occult" philosophies, it is common to find the most outrageous statements being made along these lines, causing the general public, or at least its more intelligent section, to regard the occult teachings with a certain amount of contempt. Of course, many uncritical followers of such teachings regard this contempt as something which must be borne by those who are different in their outlook from the uninstructed and prejudiced outer world. It is true that such criticism is very often both vituperative and superficial, a mental defence-weapon used by the critic to avoid the possibility of his having to revise the whole of his mental outlook; a task which we none of us care about! In matters like this it is fatally easy to allow such a bias to creep unnoticed into our thinking, and the manifest animosity and the unfairness so often displayed by the hostile critic, evoke a similar response from the believer. A very interesting example of this is to be found in the contents of the many books which have been written in connection with what we have come to be known as "The Dead Sea Scrolls". At the same time, of course, it is quite possible that a perfectly true claim to an ancient origin might be made by an esoteric school, for many of these schools, at least in the West, were forced by persecution to "go underground" and to transmit their teachings in secret.

It is necessary that we should make a clear distinction between mystery-mongering secrecy on the one hand, and legitimate reserve in communicating training and teaching to the outside world on the other. It is interesting to note that certain knowledge once held by the occult schools alone, is now being extensively used by American advertising agencies. More and more the new psychological practice is being misused and perverted by unscrupulous people, and the esotericist can point to this as a vindication of his practice of reserve in communication.

If the enquiring student should join any of the true occult schools, he will in all probability find that in the "Mythos" of the lodge, certain claims to the antiquity of its teachings will be made, but such claims, substantiated in some cases by good documentary evidence, are not put forward to the general public.

*The esoteric lodges, insofar as they are working efficiently, and producing results, do so by virtue of function, rather than charter.*

A teaching or philosophy, if it is to be of any real service must, by its very nature, conform to the description given by Jesus to the Kingdom, "The Kingdom of Heaven," He said, "is likened unto a wise householder, who bringeth forth out of his treasure things new and old."

A teaching is no less worthy of respect because it was formulated today, than is a traditional teaching going back two thousand years or more. The body of teaching is constantly being re-interpreted and illuminated by the work of the present time.

There is a *Corpus Hermeticus,* a body of teaching "once for all delivered" to the followers of the esoteric tradition by teachers from another evolutionary scheme than our own, or so it is declared in the lodges, but this foundation has been built upon and modified by generations of initiates. Like some of the great abbeys and cathedrals of this country, it shows the marks of its composite building. If we may continue to use the analogy of ecclesiastical architecture, we may say that we find in the esoteric tradition portions which suggest the first "wattle and daub" churches alongside the rough axe-hewn wooden structures of the Saxon "house-church", the heavy squat buildings of the later Saxon and early Norman periods; the soaring Gothic of the early Middle Ages (and the various modifications thereof), till we come to the banal Victorian "Gothic" reconstruction, and the experiments in steel and concrete of the present day.

It remains to be seen, of course, how much of the modern expression can be blended into the more traditional teachings which reflect the modes of thought of ancient times still forming part of the tradition, whilst, at the same time, an intense effort is being made to re-interpret tradition in terms of the present day.

Now this is typical of any living organism, this power to adapt to new conditions whilst retaining its own individuality, and it is certainly in line with the Qabalistic teaching as we have received it. *For the Qabalah is not only a body of teaching derived from the "Masters in Israel"; it is a method of using the mind in a practical and constantly widening consideration of the nature of the universe and the soul of man.*

We may say that the Qabalah was first deliberately *infolded* into the Hebrew Scriptures by the heirs of the esoteric tradition, whence, strengthened and modified by the tributary streams of Egyptian, Chaldean and Hellenic esoteric teachings, it became the Secret Wisdom of Israel, handed down from initiate to pupil through the ages.

It was the task of the "Master in Israel", the initiate of the Hebrew Mysteries, to receive and transmit the keys of this hidden wisdom in such a way that the pupil, reading in the orthodox Scriptures of his race, might unfold from their depths the secret teachings which had been folded within them. By meditation upon these teachings, and by the use of the prescribed technique, the initiate worked with this hidden wisdom, adding to it the results of his own researches, and in turn transmitting it, enlarged and enriched, to his own pupils.

Sometimes, of course, such individual work was faulty and out of line with the main tradition, but this the pupil could correct by using the glyph of the Tree of Life in the prescribed manner.

It will be seen from the foregoing that the Qabalistic system is not merely a body of knowledge, though of course it is that in part, neither is the Tree of Life a diagram in the ordinary sense of the word. Although both knowledge and diagrammatic representation are important and integral parts of the Qabalah, it is primarily, as we have already pointed out, *a method of using the mind* in such a way that the initiate comes into direct contact with the living powers and forces of the universe, and through them with the eternal source of all manifestation.

So the system of the Qabalah, though primarily an "occult" system, culminates in an exalted mysticism, and in so doing becomes a true and living theosophy.

In the same way, by the use of the sacred Scriptures of the old and new Testaments alike, the Qabalist maintains contact with the group-souls of the western races, and becomes able to influence the destinies of the West, not, it should be observed, by external political means, but by infusing into the racial unconscious seed-atoms of thought which will bear fruit in the future.

The true initiate influences the world not only by what he *says,* but, in a far more important way, by what he *is.*

It remains now to conclude this chapter by a brief account of the history of the Qabalah as far as it has become known to the scholars of the western world. The word QBL, from which the name "Qabalah" is formed, signifies "from mouth to ear", that is to say, it was an unwritten tradition passed down from one generation of initiates to another in an unbroken line. Contrary to the generally accepted opinion of Western scholars, such oral transmission can be very accurate indeed, as the present writer found when studying these matters in India. But there always comes a time when some part of the oral teaching is written down either in the form of private manuscripts which are circulated amongst the brethren, or else as an attempt to interest and attract the general public.

Scholars who have studied this question of the historical, written Qabalah, have come to certain general conclusions, though, as in all scholarly assessments of history, they disagree considerably amongst themselves! A general pattern emerges, however, and it is this pattern which we will now briefly discuss.

The two books which are the chief Qabalistic publications, are the *Sepher Yetzirah,* or Book of Formation, and the *Zohar,* or Book of Splendour. Of these the *Sephir Yetzirah* is the older, and its authorship has been attributed to Rabbi Akiba ben Joseph, a pupil of one of the contemporaries of Rabbi Gamaliel, of whom we read in the Acts of the Apostles. How far any prior esoteric teaching is embodied in the *Sepher Yetzirah* is a matter of opinion amongst scholars; but from other sources than the purely exoteric, historical ones, we are inclined to think that the author, whoever he may have been, *did* incorporate to some extent in the *Sepher Yetzirah* a very considerable amount of tradition which was coloured by Egyptian and Chaldean esoteric teachings assimilated during the Captivities.

However, as far as the *Sepher Yetzirah* is concerned, it did not appear in a published form until the sixteenth century, and it was the *Sepher Zohar,* the Book of Splendour, which first attracted attention in the West. Hostile critics have said that Rabbi Moses Shem Tov de Leon wrote this book in the thirteenth century. On the other hand, over-zealous occultists have claimed that the Book of Splendour descends from an unknown antiquity. The truth probably lies, as usual, between the two extremes.

The personal view of the present writer is that Moses de Leon edited a large number of floating manuscripts, some of which originated long before the Christian era, while others were elaborated during the most fertile Talmudic period, and that the core of this collection had been formed, (again from pre-existing and ancient sources) by Rabbi ben Jochai in the region of the Roman Emperor Antoninus, A.D. 86-161.

There is much in the *Zohar* which is evidently the result of the working of its editor's mind, a mind coloured by the accepted ideas and theories of his day, and this, of course, allows his hostile critics a good deal of scope for their attacks.

But even in our modern world, the influence of an editor still shows itself in that which he edits, and it is difficult to see how this can be entirely avoided.

Some critics have maintained that de Leon gained a living by transcribing large numbers of the *Zohar,* and squandering the profits so obtained in riotous living. However, as Waite points out, if he transcribed this large book very frequently, he would have needed a number of copyists, and the profits thereby obtained would have been so considerably reduced, that he would not have had much to squander. On the other hand, if he transcribed it by his own efforts, he would not have had time to squander the profits.

In all probability he *did* gain some profit from his editorial work (perhaps an unknown patron was behind the work) but profit may not have been his sole motive. As for the alleged neglect of his family, there may have been a certain spice of truth in this; considerably enlarged upon by his ill-wishers. It does happen in similar circles today!

It is, however, well to remember that in the time of Moses de Leon, there were in existence many other related traditions which had come down from antiquity. The *Zohar* is not the only source. How much of the wisdom of the hidden sanctuaries of the ancient world is embodied in the Qabalistic works is something which, in the nature of things, we cannot determine, but it is certain that some of that wisdom has been so transmitted.

In this connection the writer learned from a friend, an initiate of a Scottish Rosicrucian fraternity, that some very definite eleventh-century Portuguese elements existed in its ritual and teaching. Certain Phoenician influences are also to be found in other Qabalistic fraternities.

It would appear, therefore, that the body of knowledge and tradition which comes to us down the ages from some of the earliest experiences and speculations of the Hebrew race, has been augmented by many tributaries. In its Jewish aspect it still expresses some of the orthodox Jewish concepts of its eleventh century recension, but it also brings with it immemorial traditions which have come to us from the Night of Time; from times long past, and, we may also suggest, from a land now lost.

This composite tradition is that with which we are concerned in this book.

# CHAPTER II

## PSYCHISM, ILLUMINATION
## AND SEERSHIP

IN the previous pages, reference has been made to what were termed "wild talents": the apparently random appearance of certain powers and faculties which are beginning to be studied by an increasing number of psychologists. True to type, these investigators have given new names to these powers and faculties, such as "Extra-sensory-perception" and "P.K." or "Psycho-Kinesis". The parapsychologists all over the world are now working on these random powers, and at least one Chair of Parapsychology has been set up in a continental university.

The subject matter for their research is obtained by working through large batches of people, usually university students, until they find those who have some wild talent. The process rather resembles the proverbial search for a needle in a haystack, and the seers of the esoteric schools, together with the psychics and mediums of the spiritualist movement, tend to regard it with a critical eye. Nevertheless, it is bringing the methods of modern science to bear upon the subject, and whatever survives that very efficient process may be regarded as being established. This is not to say, however, that the hypotheses built up on these researches necessarily give complete and satisfactory explanations of the phenomena studied. It is necessary to take into account the personal subjective bias of the investigator, and this is a more difficult task.

From the mass of information which has been obtained by the parapsychologists, one definite fact has emerged: somewhere in the mental make-up of the individual there is, what we may describe as, a "dormer window", a casement looking out upon "perilous seas, and fairy lands forlorn", as well as upon scenes of glory and light.

The question which now arises in the minds of some parapsychologists is whether these talents belong to the past or the future of the race. Are they the remnants of a primitive faculty which was superseded by the use of the more dependable method of communication by the spoken word, or are they faculties which are latent in all and are now being gradually evolved into active use?

The esoteric schools say that this question can be answered either way, all depending upon the part of the machinery of the mind which is being used. The faculties and powers usually termed "psychic" are, and always have been, part of the content of the mind; but their mode of manifestation at any time depends upon the conditions under which it takes place. All sense impressions, whether physical or super-physical, come into the waking consciousness *through* those levels of the mind which are usually known as the "subconscious" or "unconscious", and they are always coloured and altered by their journey through those levels.

This "stained-glass" effect takes place in all cases, even when the observer prides himself upon his "objective" approach to the subject of his study. Sometimes the distortion is fairly obvious, and scientific workers recognize what they call the "personal equation" in the results of their observations. But the real stained-glass distortion usually takes place in the deeper levels of the mind, and is not apparent to the observer himself.

If we apply this to the emergence of the superphysical faculties, we see that their appearance and functioning will be altered and coloured very considerably by their passage through the subconscious levels of the mind, and as they come through much deeper levels than the ordinary physical sense impressions, they will be capable of much greater distortion.

The physical mechanism through which these subtle psychic impressions reach the level of the waking self is twofold. First, there is what is known as the involuntary nerve system, or, as it is sometimes called, the sympathetic nerve system. Then there is the voluntary or cerebro-spinal nerve system, which in terms of evolution is a much newer development than the involuntary system. Now the relative activities of these two interlocking systems vary over very wide limits, but they are always involved together in all mental activity.

Some schools of thought attempt to make a sharp line of demarcation between them, but it is found that in actual practice they are always working together; only their proportions vary. One of the chief characteristics of the involuntary nerve system is that it is closely connected with the emotional nature, and is affected by alteration of the emotional tone of the individual. On the other hand, the cerebro-spinal system is directly affected by the thoughts generated by the waking consciousness. Under normal conditions the voluntary cerebro-spinal system should be master, and the involuntary system should be the servant, but this is a counsel of perfection, for in the majority of humanity, the emotional energies tend, in varying degree, to dominate the decisions of consciousness. There is a minority in which the mental processes have, as it were, been cut off from the emotions, but this leads to the arid and sterile mentality which is so characteristic of that minority.

It will be seen, therefore, that any psychic impressions coming into consciousness will be distorted and coloured in a varying degree by the composite emotional-mental nature. Where the emotional nature predominates, the psychic processes will be largely channelled through the involuntary system, and will be haphazard and fluctuating and not under the control of the will. This is the so-called "negative" psychism, characteristic of savages, uneducated people and animals. The type of psychism associated with the voluntary nerve system is known as the "positive" psychism and in order that this type may function, its possessor must have a degree of mental development and control.

This control over its manifestations is the point which is stressed by those who have adopted a somewhat doctrinaire attitude to the development of the psychic faculties. There are, however, varying degrees of control (no psychic is always capable of full control) and even the so-called "positive" psychic can, under certain conditions, move towards the negative end of the scale. The degree of this shift will depend upon the workings of the sub-conscious levels of the mind of the psychic.

At the other end of the scale, the negative psychic is directly affected by the subconscious content of his mind, and his observations on the inner levels will always be strongly affected by the contents of his subconscious.

If allowance is made for this distortion, he may be able to do quite good work along these lines, and be of considerable assistance to his fellow men. Unfortunately however, there is a tendency for the negative psychic to become the focal point of an admiring group of people, and any criticism of his powers is regarded by that group as a heresy, a falling away from the wonderful teachings which are being received through the psychic oracle. This tends to suppress that healthy self-criticism which is the best safeguard in these subjective regions.

It does happen, occasionally, that such a negative psychic determines to change over to the more positive form of his powers, and, if he can escape from the mental grip which is exerted on him by his group, he may proceed to take the training which is necessary for this change.

His first test comes when, to his dismay, his psychic powers disappear entirely, and, as one such person told the writer, "I was as psychic as a brick wall for over two years." Because of this temporary loss of power, many negative psychics attempting to move over to the positive use of their powers are daunted and fall back to their old way of working. This is to be understood, but if they *had* persevered, they would have found that their powers would have returned, but in a new and improved form.

It is the rule of the esoteric schools to require their initiates to strive toward the positive control of the incarnationary personality, and this control includes control over the inherent psychic faculties. For this reason they do not welcome into their ranks those psychics who are the product of the ordinary "developing circle" where the habitual use of the negative forms of psychism has been firmly established. If such people are admitted, then two things tend to happen. The increased mental activity consequent upon the training which is received tends to focus the consciousness on the mental levels, and the cerebro-spinal machinery; the psychism, which has been working through the involuntary nerve system, then tends to die away; this process is deliberately accelerated by the special exercises which such initiates receive. In the Eastern schools, such negative psychics are usually not admitted, but much depends upon the individual circumstances.

Psychism, in both its positive and negative ranges, is very largely a *pictorial* consciousness, since the subconscious levels of the mind through which it works were developed in a period of evolution when language, as we understand it, did not exist. By the term "pictorial" we understand not only the visual, but also the auditory and other sense images. Now these images, or rather the stock of them which exists in the subconscious mind, are used by the psychic machinery, and, as we have said, they distort and falsify the information which is received from supernormal sources. Unless there exists a better set of images in the psychic's mind, this state of affairs will persist.

Whatever psychic impressions are received will be referred to corresponding images in the mind, in exactly the same way as, when something familiar is mentioned in ordinary conversation, the tendency is to relate the idea to our own already established knowledge of the subject in question. So, for instance, when in the course of conversation someone refers to his dog, the dog is immediately linked up in the listener's mind with the memory of his own dog. The first dog may be different in every way from the second, but until further information is supplied the listener will tend to think of it under the terms of his own memory picture.

This action of the mind is still more apparent when the subject under discussion is of a more abstract nature, especially when it is entirely new to the person concerned. Then corresponding images arise which may, or may not, correctly represent the actual subject of discussion. Such images tend, with practice, to become stereotyped, and are built into a system of thought reaction which may be flexible or the reverse. Now, this same mental machinery is used when the knowledge is being received through the operation of the psychic senses, and here difficulties begin. The incoming psychic impressions are twisted by this rigid reference-frame of the mind, and the result is a distorted and inaccurate perception. But because, when the psychic senses are working in the conscious mind, there comes, with the psychic impressions, a rush of energy from the deeper levels, such perception tends to be regarded as sacrosanct, something which must not be questioned, and this often leads to considerable trouble. The psychic feels that the energy which comes with the perception is a proof that such perception is true, *in the form under which he perceives it,* and strongly resents any attempt to criticize it.

As previously indicated, such a psychic tends to become the focusing point of a group which is attracted and held by the teachings, and there is built up a body of knowledge heavily coloured by the mental reference-frame of the psychic concerned. This effectually prevents any new knowledge, which may appear to alter the teaching, from getting through the psychic's mind. Also, by a curious telepathic compulsion, emanating from the group-mind concerned, the psychic is prevented from rising to any greater heights of perception than those already gained by him.

Since this use of *some* sort of reference-frame would appear to be inescapable, the esoteric schools have devised a frame which has the advantage of being sufficiently flexible to allow for the reception of new knowledge. This particular reference also has the virtue of disciplining the minds of group members, and therefore lessens the grip of the group-mind upon the psychic who is its focal point. This flexible reference-frame is the glyph of the Tree of Life with its associated philosophy, and it is around this "mighty all-embracing glyph of the universe and the soul of man" that both the theory and practice of the Western tradition is arranged. It is true that there are elements in the Western tradition which do not derive from the Qabalah of the Hebrews (Celtic and Iberian contacts amongst others) but it is the glory of the Tree of Life that it may be used as a kind of occult Rosetta Stone. When it is so used, then the symbols and glyphs of these other systems may be interpreted and, in fact, incorporated into the general Qabalistic picture.

By this flexible pattern of images and symbols it becomes possible to avoid, to a great extent, the distortion of the psychic perception. When the incoming psychic impressions reach this mental sieve, they are able to illuminate the symbols and so convey the essential nature of that which is being perceived on the inner levels of consciousness. This process of picking up and utilising suitable symbol forms is technically termed "illumination", and leads on to a true, but formless, direct perception in physical consciousness. This is known as "seership". There is a world of difference between the vague "sensings" of the negative psychism and the clearcut, but formless, perception of the well-developed and trained insight of the positive seer. It is only fair to say, however, that this direct perception is a rare thing. Under adverse conditions most seers tend at times to descend to the level of "illumination" or even, if these conditions are very disturbed, to descend still further and function on the "sensing" levels of the negative psychism.

All that can be done by anyone working in these higher reaches is to keep the mind directed towards the ideal of true seership, and in the meantime to work at the task of so training his mind that he becomes increasingly independent of external conditions.

From what has already been said, it will be seen that the lower psychism, when not merely "impressional", is a state of consciousness characterized by images. It is a pictorial type of perception. This is because it relates, as we have seen, to that period in evolution when the subconsciousness was predominant, this aspect of the mind being a simple picture consciousness.

Man is essentially creative, and his thought activities, in the main pictorial, have built innumerable picture-images in the collective unconscious of the human race. It is these images, the "creations of the created", as they are called, which are first observed when the psychic faculties become active, and it is only later in his training that the psychic begins to work without them. Even then, the great archetypal images of the collective unconscious influence and colour his vision, and it requires a great deal of hard work to attain to the relatively formless vision of the seer.

Here again, the glyph of the Tree comes to his aid. The picture-consciousness of the emerging faculty is brought through and conditioned by the inter-related symbol system of the Tree. Even when the psychic perceptions are inaccurate, this will be indicated by the fact that the symbolism does not agree with the basic symbolism of the Tree. The psychic will then know that the vision is inaccurate, and will take steps accordingly.

It will be clear, from the foregoing, that definite and regular meditation on the Tree of Life is an essential part of the training of the initiate of the Western tradition.

Finally, it may be said, that in the high formless perception of the true seer, common ground is reached with those who follow the mystic way, the difference being that the seer is still working in the form worlds, even though employing a formless type of perception.

In the next chapter we will discuss that great level of life and manifestation, known to many as the "astral plane", and see the working of psychic perception at that level.

# CHAPTER III

## THE ASTRAL PLANE

WHEN the phenomena of psychism are studied, it becomes apparent that, quite apart from their manifestation in the physical world, they are working in other levels of substance, and it is with these other "inner" levels that we are concerned in this chapter.

During the centuries, the vision of both trained and untrained seers and psychics has given a picture of these inner worlds. It is difficult to compress into a brief survey all that has been observed, but it may suffice if we consider the general outline.

Observations have revealed the existence of a form of substance which is extremely fluidic and mobile, having no *direct* connection with the physical world, yet present in every atom of physical matter. It has been known by many names, but the most common name in the Western tradition is "the astral light", or, in Theosophical terminology, the "astral plane". In the Orient it is usually referred to as the *Kamic* or "Desire World". In both these traditions, however, it is associated with what is known as the "mental" or *Manasic* world, and it is held that both these two attributes of sentient consciousness, desire and mind, are woven into a common world which is usually known as the "astro-mental" or *Kama-manasic* world.

We have, therefore, to picture this astro-mental world as a plane or level of fluidic mobile substance, through which currents of energy flow. In it there dwell intelligences of many kinds and grades, ranging from the lowliest types of consciousness up, through many intervening grades, to the mighty Intelligences who, from these inner levels, bear rule over all earthly manifestations, and beyond them to the in-dwelling life and consciousness of the planet itself.

Furthermore, it is held, again from what has been obtained through the use of exalted seership, that the emotional and mental aspects of all life on this planet are part of the corresponding aspects of these inner plane intelligences, and behind them, permeating, and indeed maintaining in existence all these lives and forms, is the Immanent Logos, the "Lamb slain from the foundation of the world", by whose enduring sacrifice the world is nourished and sustained.

It is sometimes stated, by critics who apparently know very little about it, that the esoteric philosophy is one of "pantheism", identifying the Creator with His creation. This is not so, for in the Western tradition the

Deity is always thought of as being both Immanent: sacrificed in His Universe, and Transcendent: reigning supreme over all.

Esoteric teaching declares that the astro-mental realms interpenetrate the physical world and also extend spatially far beyond it. At the same time, it is stated (and this has been verified by many seers), the substance of that plane is not physical substance as we know it, but one which exists in that space-time continuum which has been given the popular name of the "fourth-dimension". This means that the matter of the inner planes is not governed by the same natural laws as the dense physical world, for, like every other level of existence, it has its own definite laws of being: if it is studied from the standpoint of these laws, then all its manifestations and phenomena are seen to be as orderly as those of the physical world. For this reason the esotericist does not speak of the "supernormal", for he holds that there is but one supernatural aspect of all manifestation: the Logos from whom all Nature on all planes has its origin, and in whom all the observed sequences which we term "natural law" eternally subsist. From this standpoint, it is usual to refer to all manifestations of inner plane activity as being "supernormal" but *not* "supernatural". It will be observed that as evolution proceeds, much that is at present supernormal will come into the category of *normal* whilst, at the same time, the questing soul of man will reach out into the infinite immensities of creation and discover much more which will be studied and brought into the realms of the *normal*. There is no limit set to the range of man's mind except its inability to go beyond a certain point at any given time, and this, as it will be seen, is a constantly receding horizon.

One of the most striking qualities of this super-physical realm is the amazing mobility of its substance, and it is because of this that the practical work of the esoteric schools becomes possible. The tenuous substance of the astral light will take any form which is impressed on it by the thought of sentient beings of whatever grade; so there are built up in this realm myriads of images of all kinds. They divide naturally into two distinct groups according to their background. One group has as its background the physical world and its phenomena, whilst the other has the background of the spiritual realms beyond the astro-mental levels.

It is one of the common jeers at spiritualism that the descriptions of the "other side" which are given through mediums are so "earthly" and commonplace, and one critic has gone so far as to say that the spiritualists are "suburbanizing the cosmos".

This statement is true, but does not necessarily prove the unreliability of the seance room communicators. According to the seers "suburbanization" happens because the subconsciousness of the person who has left the physical, and now become a dweller on the astro-mental levels, automatically builds up the images of the conditions of physical life. Immediately the astral substance takes shape around these thought forms, and the man finds himself among scenery very similar to that which was around him in earth life. But since the subconsciousness has been built up according to the habitual thoughts and desires over many years, it will automatically build surrounding images which will reflect accurately the character of the man. In this way the "summerland" and the "dark spheres" and the "grey worlds", so common in spiritualist communications are built up in these finer levels.

But not only are these relatively lower levels of the astral light built up into the paradises and hells of the discarnate dwellers therein, but they are also full of the swarming images built up by the thoughts of people still in the physical body, and in this way there exists on these inner levels a great body of linked thought both consciously, and unconsciously expressed by humanity. The "collective unconscious" of the Jungian psychologists is located here, and the whole of human thinking is done in the atmosphere and under the influence of this great thought-form. Now, because man has "bodies" of the substance of the astro-mental levels, it is found by observation that there is a very real unity of the race on these levels, and that, in very fact, no man is an island.

The energy and life which is continually pouring into these inner realms, and from them into the physical world, comes from much higher levels, but manifests in these lower worlds as that energy which is known as the "libido". So, for all life on both the astro-mental and physical worlds, this driving energy is affected and conditioned by the collective subconsciousness of the race. This applies also to the animal, vegetable and mineral kingdoms, as well as to the curious halfway state which lies between the gross physical world and the levels of the astral light. This linking level, the so-called "etheric plane" of the theosophists, is of the greatest importance as we shall see when we come to deal with it. Here we are concerned with the astro-mental levels which, in their higher aspects, are its controlling factors.

The instinctive life of all the kingdoms of Nature is part of, and is controlled by, the energies of the inner levels directed by intelligences of all grades; intelligences which are themselves subject to the guiding direction of higher beings whose natural home is in the higher levels of the astro-mental world; those levels which are peopled from the spiritual realms which lie beyond them. These "group-spirits" as they are termed, form part of another aspect of the inner worlds. There is a curious pride and self-sufficiency which causes modern man to think of himself as being the only truly intelligent being in the universe, and even when considering the possibility of sentient life on other planets, he seems sure that such life will be human in form, or, if the conditions of such other words preclude this, will be inferior in some way or other to *homo sapiens*. However, with regard to the inner planes man is only one of several other lines of evolving life, and the great group-spirits of the various kingdoms of Nature belong to one or another of these independent lines of life. But because all things in this concourse of forces are linked most closely together, the intelligences of these supermundane worlds are closely linked with the whole collective thought of humanity, and inevitably act and react upon it.

It must be emphasized that the astral light is not, in itself, a plane of "form". The forms and images are derived from the mental levels which interpenetrate it. The astral light itself is a level of mobile astral substance, obeying the laws of its own nature, and is plastic in an amazing degree to the formative influence of mental activity, whether these influences proceed from incarnate or from discarnate minds. On the one hand, as the "collective unconscious" of the Jungian psychologists, it is intimately linked with the whole of life, incarnate in its varying degree on earth, and on the other it is the plastic medium through which higher intelligences fulfil the will of the Logos for the world.

It is comparatively easy to develop the power to see some of the images in the astral light, indeed, many of the brilliant little pictures which are seen by many people just before they fall asleep, or just as they awaken, the pictures termed by psychologists "hypnogogic" and "hypnopompic", are in fact the images of the astral light. It is in this region that the untrained psychic usually works, and the visions he discerns are in fact, *not* the actual astral levels, but what have been termed the "creations of the created".

In much the same way, the city dweller, if he were to live entirely in the centre of a large town, and never leave it, would see only the purely artificial urban scenery, and would know nothing of the forests and mountains, lakes and seas of the great world around, and his ideas of the world would be very inaccurate.

So it is with the untrained psychic, and therefore the esoteric schools have always insisted upon a lengthy training which would lead from psychic perception to an illuminated seership. This "higher psychism", as it has been called, works without images, but for the practical work of the schools it has been associated with the great symbol system of the Tree of Life. As we have written elsewhere, the Tree is not only a great glyph or compound symbol, *it is in essence a chart of relationships,* and, though the seer trained upon it ceases to use the symbols themselves when he reaches a certain point in his training, *the symbol-relationships still remain in his mind* and form a foundation for all his subsequent work. Other esoteric schools use other glyphs and who are we to judge . . .

Sufficient for us that in the Western tradition this is our foundation.

In the higher stages of seership "perception of" becomes "identification with" the object which is being observed, and here again, the symbol-relationship of the Tree enables the seer to bring back from those exalted regions something of what has been experirenced.

In the lower astral levels, the rolling billows of the light contain the myriad images projected by the minds of both incarnate and discarnate beings, and the astral currents energise them. In this way rhythmic influences are brought to bear upon all life, and these influences, working through the collective unconscious of the race, cause those tides in the affairs of men which are the real mainsprings of human effort for good and for bad. In very truth, the astral levels are the steering and directing levels for the race. From the lower levels come those impulses which work for the evil and unbalanced forces in human life, whilst from the higher astral come those influences which work ever towards the establishment of harmony, truth and love upon this planet.

A knowledge of these currents of energy which flow constantly behind the scenes gives the power to control and direct them, and this is part of the practical work of the esoteric craftsman. Here again, the method of the Tree is unsurpassed in its power to build up in the mind a true reference frame and a directing channel for these great energies which are constantly affecting mankind and, indeed, the myriad lives of the whole planet.

We have said that the power to control and direct the cosmic energies which are to be found in the inner planes is one which must be employed in the practical work of the occultist, but it is here that we encounter a very important pitfall. It is a commonly accepted idea that the magician has this control at his disposal and may use it in any particular way that suits his fancy or that his immediate needs may direct. Nevertheless, this is utterly false, at least as far as the brethren of the true esoteric orders are concerned. It is true that many who attempt this path *do* use the powers they obtain in order to satisfy their own personal desires and ambitions. The true esotericist, however is always mindful of the question which was put to him at the commencement of his training in the Mysteries: "Why do you desire to enter our brotherhood?" At that time he gave the answer "I desire to know in order to serve", and it is this which he must constantly remember.

But this statement, true though it is, needs some analysis. "Service" is one of those words which, like valuable currency, can be, and often is, debased. As the late Dr Joad would have said, "It all depends on what you mean by 'service'." The word has come to have several different meanings, and it is essential that we consider what it means in the context of esoteric training. Service may be given to our fellow men, to the master Craftsmen of the Order and to the Eternal. It may also be given to ourselves. Which is the true service? In point of fact, all are legitimate ways of service; it is the priorities which really matter. In what order do we place our respective services? Let us start by considering the last one I have named, the service of the self.

It is usual in many esoteric schools, more particularly those which are inclined towards the mystical rather than the true esoteric path, to despise and attempt to disregard the personal self and its requirements in a mistaken following of certain mystical teachings. The trouble with so many people is that they *will* wrench from their context certain statements made by the great teachers of the spiritual way. This is a case in point. It is quite true that at a certain point in the esoteric training, the "flyer", which is the personal self, must be immersed in the "sea" of the deep self, but this is not until a certain level of true spiritual development has been reached. It is this attempt to mortify the personality which can so easily become one of the greatest stumbling blocks on the way, so it may be as well if we consider it fairly carefully.

What is this personal self with which we mostly identify ourselves? And what is its purpose? The name itself comes from a root which means "a mask", and this recalls the actors of classic times, who represented their part in the play by wearing a mask. So they spoke "through the mask".

In the same way, so the esotericists claim, the deep self of everyone speaks and acts through the *persona,* the mask of the personal self. But this mask is not something which can be put on at leisure and dispensed with at will. It is far more than that. It is the true expression of the deep self working in the conditions of earthly time and space, and with the innumerable influences of race, heredity and custom, all of which tend to distort and alter this wonderful instrument of the self. So we may say, that this personality has what the psychologists term a "false ego", a centre around which it has been built up, but which must at a certain point be given up. *This* is the "life" which must be given up and lost in order that the Aeonian life may be gained. But all things in their order. Before the personality can be given up in this way, it must first have been developed to its utmost. Only the best is to be offered to the Lord, and many so-called "mystics" would do well to follow the teaching of one of the characters in the Bible: "We will not offer to the Lord that which has cost us nothing."*

Let us now consider the service which the esotericist should give to his fellow men. What kind of service should this be? It is commonly thought that the more obvious ways of social service are the ways through which

* II Samuel, xxiv, 24.

the race can be helped: such as lecturing to, or perhaps teaching those who are interested is what is required? Now all this is true: these are all ways of service, and for those who are capable of doing whatever is involved in them, they are true and legitimate methods of service. However, as Christ said so long ago, although these things should not be left undone, there is something else which comes first. The esotericist has always to remember that very truly, "no man is an island". He is linked with the whole of his race in the deeper aspects of his nature, and all he says, thinks or does influences the group mind of humanity. So everyone by simply being himself affects all men, but, in the case of the dedicated and trained occultist, this influence is more definite and potent for good. So the occultist helps humanity by simply being himself, and acting as it were, as a ferment which, unseen but very potent, can cause a vital change in conditions around.

We now come to that aspect of service which has gathered so much that is foolish and puerile in human thought: the service given to the adepts and masters of the esoteric way. In modern occult writings this idea of the "masters" and adepts has been so bowdlerized that it has become unacceptable to serious thinkers. "Humanity dearly loves a lord", and we have seen, in the appearance of Fascism and the National Socialism of Hitler's Germany, how a great number of people are prepared to allow others to do their thinking for them. They appear to be afraid of attempting to direct their own lives, gladly leaning upon those who will do their thinking for them, who will show them, and if needs be, drive them along the path which they must follow.

When this attitude of mind is brought to the work of esoteric science, it can easily become a form of spiritual slavery every whit as evil as any material bondage. This is the last thing that is desired by the adepti. They require mature men and women (though it is well to notice that maturity is not always a matter of age) who will stand upon their own feet, and not depend in a pathological manner upon their superiors. It is here that the terms which are in popular use encourage such dependence. The words *chela* and *guru,* which are so often used in the eastern esoteric systems are usually translated as "pupil" and "teacher". This of course would be quite a legitimate translation if the pupil-teacher relationship of the oriental systems and the pupil-teacher relationship of western education, meant the same thing to the understanding of the average person. But much of the oriental esoteric training is based upon a system of discipleship which is foreign to the psychological approach of the western mind, and, it is only fair to add, the methods of training of the true esoteric schools of the East do not encourage the servile subservience which is characteristic of so many Hindu aspirants.

However, though the true esoteric teachers do not desire any slavish obedience from their followers, they *do* require that the aspirant should "obey the rule". Here we come to something which will be familiar to those of my readers who have any knowledge of the monastic orders in the Christian church. The communities of monks or nuns live and work "under obedience", and many Protestant critics of the system seem to imagine that the members of these communities vow implicit obedience to the head of the particular monastery or convent in which they happen to be. This is not true. Obviously, there must be a system of discipline, no community can be run without some form of control, but the obedience which is demanded of the novice when taking his final vows is obedience to the "Rule of the Order", and by this Rule all the community, from the highest to the lowest, are bound.

If we take one of the orders, the Benedictines, as an example, we find that the whole life of the community is regulated by the Rule which was first laid down by the founder of the Order, St Benedict, and this rule is administered by a willing collaboration between all the brethren. Any arbitrary action by the head of the community can be challenged without fear by any brother who feels that in this instance the Rule was not being obeyed.

So in the esoteric schools the true obedience is given to the Rule of the Order which is behind the outer school. For the esoteric schools are pendant from the great orders which exist behind the scenes. Some may think that this makes membership of an esoteric school still more doubtful than they had already thought, but as the Order Rule is always taught, and can thus be compared with the general moral and ethical outlooks, the individual is always in a position to judge its validity, as far as his own capacity permits.

But any arbitrary alteration in the training methods is not permitted by his superiors. The disciplines laid down must be carried out, they are part of the training, and the individual has to realize this. At the same time, his teachers are always willing to help him in any difficult points, and he, in his turn, is expected to use his own mind in endeavouring to understand such difficulties. It must always be realized that discipline implies following the Rule freely and willingly, not in the spirit of a recalcitrant mule!

Finally we come to the greatest form of service: the service of the Eternal. Here there are two distinct stages, both of which are essential. In the first stage there is a steady endeavour to lift the personal consciousness to some measure of contact, however slight, with the eternal power, love and wisdom. From the very beginning of his training the esoteric apprentice is taught to make this effort, and to offer himself "spirit, soul and body as a living and continual sacrifice". In the ritual of the Qabalistic Cross he says with gesture and word *Ateh, Malkuth, ve Geburah, ve Gedulah le Olam:* "To Thee is the Kingdom, the Power and the Glory, for ever and ever."

Persisting in this, there come, in the course of his training and the development of the inner faculties, "illuminations" on "the mount" and in the light of these he learns to look at all life from another point of view, *sub species eternitas,* and so discern, on the tracing board of the Architect of the Universe, the plan which is the basic of all evolutionary existence. Now he must learn to descend the mount, and coming into the field of ordinary life, endeavour to live and work under the precepts of the Will which ordered that plan. Only then can the aspirant find true happiness and rest. As the blessed souls told Dante, "In His will is our peace." So in the end, the path of esoteric science merges into the path which is common to mystic, occultist and Nature-mystic alike. And as, in the Holy Mysteries, the gifts of bread and wine which are the representations of the offerings and sacrifice of the people are mystically offered on the heavenly altar and thence returned to the earthly altar as the means whereby the faithful may receive the very life and power of the eternal, so in this personal offering of the self, and the illumination and power which results therefrom, the aspirant begins to work with true power and right knowledge of the lower worlds. Only then is the service of the eternal realized and fulfilled by him, and in that service he finds that "perfect freedom" which is referred to in the old Anglican collect.

# CHAPTER IV

# MODERN PSYCHOLOGY

IT is not proposed to discuss the details of modern psychological theory, since, unlike ancient Gaul, it is divided into many more parts than three. The many schools of psychology stem, in the main, from the three systems identified with the names of Freud, Adler and Jung.

The chief way in which these modern psychological theories differ from the academic psychology of the nineteenth century is that they immensely extend the concept of the self of man. The older psychology dealt with man as an entirely conscious being, an "encapsulated entity", whose conscious thoughts, emotions and aspirations constituted his entire psychological make-up.

With the rise of many unorthodox philosophical and religious movements, and more particularly modern spiritualism and theosophy, it became necessary, once the facts had been established, to try to fit them into the existing psychological framework. It was then found that the framework itself would need much alteration and adjustment if it were to cover all the new aspects of the mind of man which were now being revealed.

It is to the scholar and investigator of psychic happenings, F. W. H. Myers, that we owe the concept of what he named the "subliminal mind". The word comes from "limen" meaning a threshold. To Myers, and those associated with him, the conscious mind was pictured, not as the whole mind, but merely as a part of it. To them it seemed to be only the ground floor of the mental structure; the threshold, as it were, of the whole edifice. Above it, and below it were other levels of mental activity, and with these, so far as mental control was concerned, the conscious mind had very little to do. Nevertheless, the influence and direction from these levels was constant, so Myers spoke of the "subliminal" and "supraliminal", and, although at first this latter term was used simply to refer to the waking conscious self, it came to be regarded in another way at a later date.

Myers did not, at first, attempt to differentiate between the levels of the subliminal mind, but others began to work with his ideas and evolved the concept of the "subconscious" aspects of the mind.

Much of the general body of new psychological theory, bitterly opposed, as it was, by the conservative "psychologists" of his day, was expanded and given a new look by the pioneering work of the great psychologist Freud. When his theories first burst upon the world they received so lopsided a welcome that they became suspect to many people; to explain why this should have happened it will be necessary to discuss briefly some of his main ideas.

Freud was a medical psychologist and during his work with his patients he began to formulate certain ideas in order that he might explain to them the abnormal workings of the minds of mental sufferers; at the same time he saw that much of the behaviour of the minds of normal people could be accounted for in this way. He found, as Myers and many others had done, that the region of the mind which lay below the threshold of consciousness, the subliminal or "subconscious", was affected by every impression received by way of the five senses. All such impressions, *and the emotions and thoughts evoked by them,* were registered in the depths of this mental level.

Since, however, there exists a certain code of conduct, many of these emotions and thoughts were not acceptable to the conscious mind, and there came into existence, what was termed the "endo-psychic censor". The function of this censor was to prevent unacceptable expressions of this nature from rising up from the subliminal realms, and so affecting the conscious self. It was a kind of one-way sieve which, while it allowed all impressions to pass down into the depths of the subconscious, prevented the return of those thoughts and emotions that were not acceptable to the personal consciousness.

But "out of sight" was very definitely *not* "out of mind", for Freud discovered that these unwanted emotions and thoughts were very much alive and active in the subliminal depths, and (a most important point), that they were constantly affecting the waking consciousness. Working with his patients, he found that all such subconscious impressions were under a constant pressure from forces which were entering the mind at its deepest levels. These forces were differentiations of a dynamic energy which was the sustaining power of the whole personality, the *élan vitale* of Bergson. This primary "thrust of life" was named "libido", and it was here that Freud made his most valuable and spectacular discoveries. He claimed that the inflowing energy split up into three main streams, and that these streams were the forces behind the three "instincts" of self-preservation, sex, and herd.

It was in the realm of the second instinct, sex, that his main contribution lay, and, of course, it was this bias which gave his ideas a notoriety that, to some extent, was not deserved. Sex, in the popular mind, means something very definite and limited, but Freud used the term to cover a much wider field, embracing, as it did, all the manifold expressions of the creative instinct of which physical sex is only one part.

He evolved a technique which he found made it possible to gain admission to the depths of the subconscious and to study its workings. This technique ("psycho-analysis"), by word association tests and the study of the patient's dreams, enabled him to penetrate behind the "censor" and bring hidden mental material into consciousness. When this was done, he found that a great deal of emotional energy, which had been locked up in these hidden thought complexes, was released with beneficial results to the patient. Freud also discovered that certain hidden thought complexes tended to split off from the main mental stream and become semi-independent. Such "dissociation" was liable to have very serious consequences, for these dissociated complexes could radically alter the whole of the sufferer's personality. Classic cases such as "The Watseka Wonder" and the "Sally Beauchamp" multiple personality case (and, in more recent times, that of Evelyn Lancaster whose history has been given to the public in the books entitled *The Three Faces of Eve* and *Strangers in My Body*) show to what lengths "schizophrenia" can go.*

It became evident to Freud and his co-workers that one of the factors which cause dissociation in its various forms was the repression into the subliminal depths of much that offended the normal standards of the waking self. Rather than admit that certain thoughts and emotions were self originated and natural, the waking self refused to acknowledge them, or to allow them to pass into the conscious mind. Instead they were repressed into the subconscious limbo, where they locked up the inflowing nervous energy or deflected it into abnormal channels. When the complexes were uncovered, it was held by Freud that the mind would revert to normality, and in many cases this did occur.

However, two of Freud's associates, Alfred Adler and Carl Gustav Jung, felt that Freud's insistence on sex as the chief factor in mental illness was not entirely justified, and they began to move away from that standpoint and to form their own schools of thought. Adler laid great stress upon the "power complex", teaching that this manifestation of the self-preservation instinct was responsible for a great deal of mental disturbance attributed by Freud to sex. If results are a criterion, they have proved him to be correct, and the psychologists of his school have done a great deal of very good work.

However, Jung, in the present writer's opinion, stands out from his two illustrious confrères by the magnificent sweep of his system of psychology; he also comes nearer than either of the others to the viewpoint of the Qabalists. Briefly, it may be said that Jung recognizes the existence

---

* *The Three Faces of Eve* — Drs Thigpen & Cleckley — Published 1957. *Strangers in My Body* — Evelyn Lancaster — Published 1958 Secker & Warburg, London.

of what has been termed the "libido", a force of which all physical, or life forces, are manifestations. This living energy flows between the two poles: the "conscious" and the "unconscious" aspects of the personality. If, for any reason, the conscious self fails to hold its requisite amount of this libido, then at whatever point this deficiency occurs, there will be found an excess of energy in the unconscious. Whenever the living energy projects itself from the unconscious depths, (the matrix or primal source from which, or through which, it flows into the human personality), it is to be found expressing itself as a grouping of opposites. Here we have in another form that which is expressed in the Qabalistic conception of the two pillars of the Tree of Life, headed by the *Sephiroth Chokmah* and *Binah.*

Freud regarded the unconscious levels of the mind as the limbo into which were jettisoned emotions, thoughts and memories which were objectionable to the conscious self.

This Jung was ready to admit, but from his own researches he came to the conclusion that there were other things in the unconscious. One of these was the deposit of the experiences of our ancestors, and he called this the racial or collective unconscious. The conscious mind is held to be the outcropping of the unconscious, just as the visible portion of the iceberg is the outcropping of the greater mass of ice which lies below. An even better analogy is that of the mountain range. The individual pinnacles can be held to represent individual consciousnesses, the peaks would then represent the racial consciousness of the various nations and human groupings, whilst the great body of the range would represent the animal and vegetable life of the planet. All these are joined together by their common base and origin: the earth itself.

If the conscious mind is an outgrowing from the underlying unconscious, then the springs of life are to be found in it, and the "libido" is seen to be not only an inflowing energy, blindly thrusting up into consciousness, but also a *directive* force which has certain characteristics.

This directive energy is a steady pressure in the direction of progression, here defined as the feeling that "things are moving", indicating that the conscious self has opportunities and possibilities which may be brought into manifestation. But such a feeling can produce a one-sided attitude towards life. The everchanging circumstances of the world around demand a flexible approach by the mind; when a rigid one-sided outlook prevents this, the individual "gets into a groove", as we say. Somewhere, in *The Professor at the Breakfast Table,* Oliver Wendell Holmes remarks that the only difference between a groove and a grave is their respective depth.

In the psychological field this certainly holds good, for the inflowing life is so constricted by this mental attitude that its course is deflected and various forms of mental illness appear. The most spectacular of these is extreme mental dissociation such as that already referred to in the case of Evelyn Lancaster, but very many lesser forms of mental ill-health abound on every side of us.

One of the ways in which the libido reacts to such inner conflicts is to withdraw into the depths of the personality. This means that the conscious self is deprived of much of the vital force which it needs, and becomes impotent in the affairs of life; fighting where it should be diplomatic, being diplomatic where it should be fighting, and at the same time unable to carry any such attitude to the point where it could really be of use. But the regression of the libido into the unconscious depths causes it to bring certain healing power to bear, and when the latent energies become sufficiently strong, they may emerge into the field of the conscious mind. Such an eruption of the unconscious can, when properly directed, break down much of the rigidity of the conscious self, and enable the person concerned to make new adjustments to outside circumstances. So it will be seen that there is a certain rhythm in the working of the lifeforce. There is a period of progression, then a period of regression, and this *enantiodromia,* as it was termed by Heraclitus, is a normal action of the mind. But trouble begins when the mind sticks too strongly to either pole of activity.

Now there are many things in the unconscious levels which relate to the early primitive attitudes to life, and there are very many experiences in conscious life which are distasteful and repugnant to the individual. These tend to be thrust down by the "censor" beneath the threshold of consciousness, and so are prevented from being manifested in conscious thought, word and deed.

Such inhibition is a normal and necessary activity of the mind. The trouble arises when the conscious self adopts an attitude of *"All these things are below me, and I am not responsible for them.* Neither do I allow such thoughts and feelings in myself, I have put them out of my mind." Unfortunately, although such primitive outlooks may have been put out of sight, they are anything but "out of mind". They attract to themselves some of the inflowing psychical energy and are, as it were, a "resistance pocket" in the personality, constantly at war with the waking self, and constantly attempting to rise up into, and influence, the waking consciousness. In the waking life these attempts usually show themselves as irrational words or actions, for which there appears to be no apparent reason.

But it is in the sleep state that these buried complexes are able to emerge more fully, just as, in our "resistance pocket" analogy, its members were able to operate more freely in the night. So in the dream-life of the

individual these imprisoned "things" emerge into the waking consciousness in the symbolic form of dreams. In their true form they are
unable to pass the censor, but in symbolic disguise they can get by and so
emerge on to the conscious levels. Both Freud and Jung developed a
technique of dream analysis which would enable them to discover the
nature of the hidden complexes which were causing the neurotic troubles
of their patients. This, together with the method of "free association", was
held by many of the early psycho-analysts to be sufficient to effect a cure.
Jung, however, not satisfied with this, held that it was not sufficient to
relieve the blocked waters of the emotional complex by breaking down the
psychic dam which had confined them. It was also necessary to cut new
channels and redirect the incoming libido in such a way that further
trouble of that kind could be avoided.

Another characteristic teaching of Jung is that men and women may be
classified with two main types, the outward-turning and the inward-
turning, the extrovert and the introvert. Pure types are rare and human
personalities can generally be classified under one or other of these
headings. Both types are representative of normal attitudes to life, but both
can develop a form of mental disease when they are carried to extremes
by a desire to escape from the stress and strain of the realities of life.

In the dreams of both types there occur certain symbols which, on
investigation, turn out to be symbols which were consciously employed
in the childhood of mankind, or even, for that matter, in comparatively
recent human history, though to the average person they are usually
unknown. Such symbols appear to be very real sources of energy within
the self. They are termed "archetypes", and are held to be of the greatest
importance, since they indicate the direction in which the libido is
attempting to flow. When such symbols appear in a composite form, then
we have a glyph, or "mandala". A glyph has been defined as the coat of
arms of the forces being dealt with, and it is a normal activity of the human
personality to build up such glyphs. In neurotic and psychopathic subjects,
such glyphs appear in the dream state, or arise spontaneously in the
waking life, and they indicate the nature of the forces which are concerned
in the neurosis.

When we study the Tree of Life, which is a very ancient mandala, we
find that it conforms very closely to the Jungian concepts, or should we
rather say that the teachings of the school of Jung are very close to the
ancient teachings?

There are other teachings of the Zurich psychologist which cannot be
touched upon here, since they would take up too much of our space, but
it may be said that they are capable of being "placed on the Tree", i.e.,
they fit into the scheme of the mighty glyph.

There is, however, one point in the teachings of Jung which we should mention, and that is his concept of the "self". We mostly tend to identify ourselves with the ego-sense, with the "I am"; the conscious waking self. But this empiric, or false ego, is held by Jung to be something which must ultimately be discarded, or, to be more accurate, must be superseded by a new centre of consciousness which will form a point of equilibrium between the conscious and unconscious aspects of the personality.

Here again, the teaching associated with the Tree of Life insists upon this same necessity; the necessity of losing the life of the false ego in order that a fuller life may be experienced.

From all that has been said it will appear that the system of "analytical psychology" which C. G. Jung devised is very near to the teachings and practices of the arcane schools, and more particularly to those of the Qabalistic tradition.

It is obvious that such an integrated system of teaching cannot adequately be summarized in a few paragraphs, but it is hoped that sufficient will have been given to enable the reader to get some idea of the system. Perhaps we may summarize what has been written here by saying that Jung does not regard the unconscious as being only the rubbish heap of the mind, contaminating the pure waters of instinctive life as they endeavour to flow through it, and erecting all kinds of obstacles to their passage. Rather does he look to it as being also the ground and root of the conscious waking self, constantly engaged in an attempt to bring the forces of life into those channels which will allow them to fertilize and render fruitful *all* the aspects of the self. So, as Jung claimed, his system is primarily one which is concerned with the establishment of balance and reintegration in the personality.

This is also claimed to be the aim of the system of philosophy which is based upon the Tree of Life — the mighty, all-embracing glyph of the universe and the soul of man.

# CHAPTER V

## DIRECT EXPERIENCE

IT was said by them of old time, that the Mysteries gave their initiates a supreme boon: freedom from the fear of death, and although this might be somewhat doubtful in the case of the semi-public Elusinian Mysteries of Grace, it was certainly true of the deeper sanctuaries of initiation.

Of course it is equally true that a debased spiritualism, combined with a certain amount of astrology also existed in those days, and for many of those who partook in its seances it provided an intellectual proof of the existence of other realms of being apart from the purely physical. Indeed for some of its adherents it provided the same certainty of continuing life as did the more august Mysteries.

In both these cases, the operative factor which enabled this certainty to be attained was that which we have here termed "wild talent", though there was a considerable difference in its application and control as far as these two movements were concerned. But the essence of both was *direct experience*. To deduce the underlying laws from intellectual study, based upon what was observed, was one aspect which bulked largely in the true mysteries, whilst the same aspect in the public cult tended to become a *cthonic* or "underworld" cult, and became debased and contaminated by many alien elements. But common to both was this factor of direct experience of supernormal things; an experience which resulted in freedom from the fear of death. However, it is possible to lose sight of the wood because of the trees, and it was certainly so in both cases. For the over elaboration of the purely intellectual aspect often tended to eclipse this direct experience in the Mysteries, whilst the emotional cult of the underworld, with all its doubtful associations also tended to lose its power to give its followers direct experience, and so in official Mystery school and underworld seance cult alike, reliance began to be concentrated upon that which was received through the supernormal faculties of certain people who were known as seers and, in the case of the female psychics, pythonesses or oracles.

At the level of the Mysteries, the oracles of Apollo at Delphi and that of Dodona were possibly the most famous in the ancient world, whilst on the level of the cthonic cults there emerged the "wise man" and "wise woman", who, because of their psychic faculty, were regarded as sources of information beyond the normal. In both cases, however, it can be seen how great was the loss of the more general direct experience. In the official Mysteries it led to a sterile philosophizing, whilst in the underworld cults it led to internal dissensions, the followers of one psychic against the followers of another, and to the encouragement of the worst elements of human nature.

It was one of the great attractions of Christianity that it offered to all its followers some form of direct experience. Its supreme message was the work of the atoning Son of God, and the possibility of making a direct living contact with Him. Its second message was the proclamation of the Resurrection with its accompanying proof of survival beyond bodily death, and the proclamation of a new order. The powers of evil had been vanquished, and man was rescued from their thrall. This was the *kergyma,* the good news which Christianity was proclaiming throughout the world, and together with this there was an intense living faith in the presence and power of the Master.

In this atmosphere of positive faith, the small Christian communities found that the power which He had promised them, and which they held to be the Spirit of wisdom and consolation, was enabling them to have some measure of direct experience of the "things not seen". So St Paul, writing to his Corinthian converts enumerates the "gifts" or *charismata* which were being unfolded and used by the brethren, pointing out at the same time something which all great religious teachers have stressed, namely that the "spiritual gifts", as the Authorized Version of the Bible terms them, are more properly called "psychic gifts". They are not in themselves *spiritual* in what we may term the ethical meaning of that word, and as St Paul points out, they are secondary to the real thing, which is an attitude of heart and mind directed to the service, in the true sense, of God and mankind. "The greatest of these is Love," says the Apostle.

At the same time, however, this direct experience was of the greatest help to the infant church, since it afforded to all alike the possibility of some measure of individual contact with the unseen things, and as long as this possibility was recognized, the church went from strength.

With the influx into Christianity of those who had been trained in the Mysteries of the older religions, there grew up an inner teaching which, based as it was upon the Hebrew traditions and upon the inner teaching given by Christ to His Apostles, enlarged again by Grecian, Persian and Egyptian outlooks, developed into the composite movement which is known as Christian Gnosticism. This Gnostic movement has always had more than its fair share of adverse criticism. Some of this was justified (not all the Gnostic schools came up to the standard set by Christ) but others were far different and hardly deserved the venomous attacks of "Saint" Ireneus and others.

Clement of Alexandria and Origen both represent another strand in the complex web of the early Church; careful study of their writings reveals the presence in the church of an inner core of people, who not only had direct experience of inner, supernormal things, but were also heirs to that wisdom which had been transmitted through the ages from times out of mind.

With the increasing secularization of the church, and the beginnings of its entry into the political field, direct experience began to be subordinated to outer organization, and, concurrently, those who held the deeper teachings were expelled from the church, though the charismata still continued to manifest sporadically. Indeed the Venerable Bede, writing in the ninth century, though lamenting the loss of most of the "gifts" was able to say that the gifts of healing still remained. In point of fact, as we have said, the "gifts" were manifested throughout the ages, though sporadically and usually in an unregulated fashion. This applies not only to the great Catholic communions of East and West, but also to many of the heretical and schismatic sects which "hived off" from them throughout the years. Many of these, in their inception at least, had such direct experience of the inner realities. But this experience was usually without any definite framework, and was regarded as either a sign of the truth of their particular heresy or else as a sign of divine approval of the individuals who experienced it. In the great Orthodox and Roman communions, such direct experience was discouraged since the mystic temperament has a definite bias against it when received through psychical means. The mystic, whether of the East or West, seeking union with the Supreme Reality, has little time to spare in the "Vanity Fair" of either the mundane or the psychical world.

But with the rise of the scientific and enquiring "age of reason", the direct experiences of the mystics, together with the records of similar experiences given in the Scriptures, began to be subjected to the criticism of what was proudly described as the "rational" mind. It was held, erroneously, as we believe, that it was possible for human thinkers *at the present stage of their evolution,* to be able to make correct *objective* judgements of these subjective experiences. Disregarding the scriptural injunction that "He who judgeth a matter without knowledge, it is a shame and a folly unto him", the Victorian scientists regarded all records of direct experience as simply due to human credulity and self-deception.

Curiously enough, in view of the hostility of official science to the claims of Christianity, the leaders of the Anglican Church joined the rationalists in an unholy alliance against those who in any way manifested the very gifts which they should themselves been showing forth. "Enthusiasm" in any form was abhorrent to them, as instanced by the rebuke given to Wesley by an Anglican bishop.

But the clock cannot be turned back by mere suppression, and the psychical energies cannot be extinguished by the fiat of scientist or prelate. So there arose movements which were centred upon the direct experience of supernormal things. Modern Theosophy, modern spiritualism and the loosely knit organizations of the New Thought Movement all began to teach that direct experience of the inner side of things was possible.

Bitterly opposed by church and science, they have increased and established themselves, until now, in at least one instance, they are conforming to the ancient pattern, and attempting, as far as possible, to ostracize and reject those of their members who do not see eye to eye with the leaders.

But the wheel has brought to them the fruits of the seeds sown by their obscure brethren in the past: the alchemists, the Rosicrucians and many others who preserved the golden thread of direct experience. "Where there is no vision the people perish", for without direct experience the old Nature-worship degenerates into orgiastic rites; the church becomes impotent and unable to obey her Lord's command as she should, and rational philosophy and science become sterile and unable to minister to the deeper needs of the soul of man. It will be seen that there are three main paths of development which lie before the enquirer. Two of them, nature-mysticism and mysticism, are paths of the emotions, whilst the third is a path of the mind.

It is impossible, of course, to make a clear-cut distinction in actual practice, for even in the most intellectual appraisal of the universe and the soul of man it is easy to recognize the emotional undertones which lie beneath it, whilst even the most emotional of the mystics shows some elementary use of the intellect. However, these are the three main paths. They are studied in the East under the titles of *Raj* Yoga, *Bhakti* Yoga and *Gnani* Yoga. There are, of course other lines of activity, such as *mantra* yoga, *laya* yoga, *karma* yoga, etc., but these are all subsidiary methods of training which lead to one or other of the three main paths.

We are fully aware that this division of the yoga paths will be regarded by some students as "not according to Cocker", but it is based upon the author's own experience in India when working with a group of Hindu occultists, and it agrees very well with the Western system.

These paths are acknowledged and trodden by those who follow the Western Mysteries, though the path of the mind, the Hermetic Path, is held by us to be the most important. For though a man may make a living contact with the elemental powers behind Nature, and another may achieve a mystical contact with deep spiritual reality, yet, unless the mind has been trained, all the results of such contact will inevitably be distorted and misapplied on the physical plane.

On all of these ways to God, the psychic faculties show themselves, but in the Hermetic Path they are trained and developed, whereas in both the others they tend to work in a random way, and, indeed, on the mystic way they are usually regarded as hindrances rather than helps. Emotion has been regarded as something which should be reduced to a minimum as far as possible, but as modern psychology has shown, emotion is the driving force behind all human effort and development, and without it the mind of man becomes sterile and ineffective.

At the same time, of course, its unregulated manifestations can be equally disastrous. A land may become waste and uninhabitable if its water is allowed to flood all the land. True use of the source of water is made when it is controlled and directed by sluice and dam and irrigation channel. Then will the desert blossom as the rose.

It is this method of engineering, applied in the sphere of the self, which is the basis of the great glyph of the Tree of Life, the underlying principles of which we are studying. As we shall be devoting most of our time to the consideration of the Hermetic Way, it may be well if we deal briefly with the other two paths.

The path of Nature-Mysticism, the Green Ray, as it is sometimes termed, has, like the other two ways, both its advantages and its dangers. It is a path of direct experience, the experience of God made manifest in Nature. It is a living contact with the informing life of the planet and is a vitalizing element in all human life. Unless the elemental energies are contacted, to some extent at least, man is sterile and ineffective on the physical plane. Fortunately, we are compelled to make a minimal contact with these forces because of the automatic functioning of our physical bodies, but more than this is needed if we wish to live more fully.

During periods of social repression and inhibition the elemental forces tend to be throttled down and banked up behind the conscious selves of men. It is then that the repressed energy begins to seek fresh outlets, and, finding a weak point may wear the barrier away, bursting its restraints and flooding the racial consciousness, thus bringing destruction to the orderly work of the race. To prevent this, the initiates of the Green Ray open up certain channels in the racial unconscious (concerning which the great psychologist Jung wrote so eloquently), and through these channels the elemental forces, controlled and directed, pour into the soul of man. This gives a vital illumination and energy which spurs the race to new endeavours. In this country such an elemental contact was made during the reign of the first Elizabeth and there have been others of a similar kind. One outstanding example, of course, is the classical Renaissance in Europe.

Where the restraining barriers are too strong, however, it may happen that this elemental force begins to energize anew the old forms of Nature Mysticism, and the witch-cult again begins to attract its devotees. Any nation which allows these suppressions and checks on the elemental forces is a nation with a neurosis, and, such a condition, lying as it does below the conscious levels of the mind, can be a potential source of danger.

It is necessary to point out, however, that in this, as in all manifestation, there is a natural rhythm and there will be times when the elemental forces thrust forward into manifestation in the souls of men, just as there will be periods when they ebb and recede. The true initiate of the Green Ray learns to work with these tides and to control and direct them for the good of the race, but there are many people outside the ranks of the nature mystics for whom this contact is unregulated and spasmodic. This is largely true of the Celtic races and accounts for some of the inconsistencies which are so characteristic of them. When the Celt is "on his contacts", to use a technical term, he can reach up to the stars, and nothing seems impossible to him. When, however, his contact has been lost, he is moody and depressed and incapable of sustained effort.

To those who are by temperament and racial inheritance naturally drawn to it, this path of the Green Ray offers an opportunity to stabilize their physical nature, to control their contact with the elemental forces and to prevent the violent alternations of those forces from affecting them, as would otherwise be the case. It is also one of the ways, and a valid way, whereby the soul, having made contact with God made manifest in Nature, may rise to contact and ultimate union with "Him who dwelleth in light inaccessible".

Unfortunately, like all other ways, it has its obverse side, and because of this it has received more than its fair share of misrepresentation and abuse. More particularly has this been the case in those parts of the world where Christianity has been strongly entrenched in the mechanism of the state, and able therefore, to exert the utmost pressure upon those who differed in any way from its own teachings. At the same time, although this is no excuse for the enormities perpetrated in the name of the Lord of Love, this bias is understandable when one considers the conditions in which Christianity began in the Roman Empire.

Into the structure of the lore of the Green Ray there is incorporated a very profound teaching concerning the more recondite aspects of sex, and it is this which has always brought down upon the initiates of the Green Ray the enmity of orthodox Christianity. It is also, of course, this aspect of the path of the Green Ray which can so easily be distorted and misapplied, as it was in medieval times in Europe. But the abuse of a thing is no excuse for neglect of its legitimate use, although, at the same time, it is understandable that the official church, with its knowledge of the past, tried to put it down.

It is usual for those who have been trained and brought up in the classical tradition to minimize the more evil side of Roman life. Rudyard Kipling's works idealize the Roman culture in this way, but, at the same time, there was an appalling amount of evil which was part of the very warp and woof of Roman life. More particularly was this evident in the arena, where spectacles were exhibited in which some of the myths of the gods and goddesses and their relations with human beings, were enacted with absolute realism. There was no pretence, what the myth set forth was literally enacted before the thousands of spectators. Pasiphae and the Bull, the slaying of the Titans, and others of the same kind were so enacted, as the Roman writer Martial records.* In *The Golden Ass,* Apulius, writing many years later, refers to similar spectacles. It is important to remember that these things were done in full public view, not in the brothels and stews of Port Said or modern Alexandria for the attraction of European tourists of the baser class.

Because these things were so, the Christian Church reacted strongly against the whole pagan system, and in the process threw away several babies with the dirty water! Our chief difficulty in judging the early Christian period is that we tend to look through twentieth century spectacles at the pagan scene, and this attitude can be very misleading.

However, the abuse does not preclude the right use of anything, and there are aspects of sex, or, to use a more correct term "polarity", which have a very great value. It is these which are the content of some of the teachings of the Green Ray. In themselves they are of great importance and are, in a true sense, moral; their misuse however, can, and does, produce something very horrible, approximating to the spectacles of the pagan days. This is evident in some of the records of medieval witchcraft. At the same time it should be kept in mind that the methods used to extort the truth from the supposed witches were so very drastic as to invalidate much that was recorded as their "confessions", though a sufficient residue remains to show that not all the witches and wizards were the harmless natural psychics many spiritualists suppose them to have been.

However, these things are the pathologies of the Green Ray, and must not be taken as any criterion of the character and work of those who follow this Path which leads to the Light as surely as any other.

Many of its initiates have been in the forefront of artistic revival, and a renewal of aesthetic values, such as the Celtic renaissance in Ireland at the end of the last century and the beginning of this, owed much to the presence in its midst of those who followed the path of the Green Ray.

In more recent times the work of psychologists of both the Freudian and Jungian schools of thought has shown the very great importance of this contact with the elemental forces of life, and has justified the work of the Green

---

* *De Spectaculis Liber,* v. cp. Suetonius, Nero. XII 2.

Ray initiates in the Kingdom of *Adonai ha arezt,* God made manifest in Nature.

It remains to consider very briefly the path of the Purple Ray: the path of mysticism. Here we have to remember that its followers are to be found in all the great religions of the world, even as are the followers of the other ways, though the orthodox Christian churches have always tended to regard the mystical traditions of other faiths as outside the pale, so to speak, and only in recent times has there been any attempt made to study the mystical teachings of non-Christian religions. To their credit be it said that this attempt has, in the main, been made by theologians of the Roman Catholic Church.

However, the church itself has always been somewhat suspicious of the activities of the mystics in its own fold, suspecting them of leanings towards monism or pantheism, and indeed, some of the utterances of some of the mystics have encouraged this suspicion.

But on the whole the Catholic churches of both Western and Eastern obediences have been the nursing ground for the development of a definite Christian mystical tradition and practice. Islam has its mystical side in the Sufi sects, whilst in the Hindu religion the path of *Bhakti* Yoga is the path pre-eminent of its own mystics.

In the Christian churches, the path of the mystic has sometimes been known as the Threefold Way of Purgation, Illumination and Union, and there is a very considerable body of writings based upon this classification, some of which are mentioned in the bibliography at the end of this book.

Contrary to popular belief the path of the mystic is anything but a sentimental idealism and escapism. The mystic does indeed turn away from the multiplicity of things and seek the unity, but, and this is most important, it is not through any desire to escape from the difficulties and troubles of the world in order that he may himself find peace. Rather does he tread a path of high aspiration and severe discipline, seeking the unity in a passion of love and adoration in order that through him the whole world may be helped. "Selfish salvation there is none," is an old Catholic saying, and the true mystic does not seek personal salvation but rather that he may, through love and adoration, be attuned to that Will in whose service is perfect freedom.

Such an attitude is far removed from the pseudo-mysticism so current at the present time in both East and West. If any should doubt this, let them read the writings of St Teresa d'Avila, of Ruysbroek and of St John of the Cross. Therein will be found something of the spirit of the true mystic quest.

# CHAPTER VI

## ASPECTS OF THE QABALAH

THERE are several different aspects of the Qabalah, and each student will be drawn to select from these the one most suited to his temperamental bias. It is essential to remember, however, that although one aspect may be the natural line of work for one particular student, it is very necessary that he should have a fair knowledge of the others in order that his studies may be balanced. It is usual to divide the Qabalah under the following heads:

(1) The dogmatic Qabalah.
(2) The literal Qabalah.
(3) The practical Qabalah.
(4) The unwritten Qabalah.

We will not discuss these four in the order given, and, as we proceed, it will be seen that we are working from the outer presentation of the Qabalistic philosophy back to its inner essence. This has been done for two reasons. The student starts from known terms and concepts and then begins to deal with those which are different, in many ways, from his normal thinking; he will find, however, that by the time he reaches the later stages of this classification, he has begun to acquire a new set of concepts *and* a new vocabulary with which to deal with them.

Let us then begin with the dogmatic Qabalah. This is the outer doctrine which is embodied in the classical written sources of which we spoke in the first chapter of this book. It is well to remember however, that the *Zohar* and the *Sepher Yetzirsh* are not single works, but are made up of several works gathered together under those heads.

There are certain problems which any philosophy worthy of the name must attempt to solve such as the Nature and attributes of the Supreme Being, the mysteries of creation, the nature of life, and the being and destiny of man. In the dogmatic or written Qabalah these ideas are considered within a definite system of relationships and concepts known as the Tree of Life, and it is this basic relationship diagram or "mandala" (as the Easterns term such figures), which is the key to all Qabalistic teaching.

It may be helpful if we here give a fundamental principle which lies behind all Qabalistic teaching and thought: the principle of "balance". As the student proceeds in his work with the Qabalah, he will find this principle a key which unlocks many closed doors. In fact the basic Qabalistic treatise starts with the words "The Book of the Concealed Mystery is the book of the equilibrium of balance."

We come now to the second head in our classification, the "literal" Qabalah; here we enter a world of thought where the fixed landmarks of logical thought are superseded by a method which in many ways resembles the dictum of the Red Queen in *Alice Through the Looking Glass:* "When I say a thing is so three times, then it *is* so." (I quote from memory, but that is the general idea.)

The methods of the literal Qabalah have been described by one occultist, Dion Fortune, as being akin to doing mensuration with the aid of an elastic ruler, and from the ordinary point of view, this is a very apt description. These peculiar ways of mental working depend upon the fact that every letter of the Hebrew alphabet has a numerical value. This is also the case with the Greek alphabet, and the same curious method of thought can be used with that also.

There are three main methods for the deciphering of the literal Qabalah. The first with which we will deal is known as the Gematria. Here the principle is that words of a similar numerical value explain one another. Thus, the word *Achad,* meaning unity has for its number value 13, and this is also true of *Aheba,* which means Love. So Unity and Love express the same idea.

It is obvious that there are infinite possibilities in this method, but to anyone who is acquainted with modern psychological work it will also appear that there is method in the apparent madness of the ancient rabbis. This is even more apparent when we come to the next division of the literal Qabalah — *Notariqon.* Here a word is taken and each of its letters is used as the initial letter of the new word. Thus if we use our own English language, and take as an illustration the word "Man", we can by this method form the sentence "Many are near." Some of the applications of this method caused the medieval rabbis to reject the Qabalah: it was being used to convert Jews to Christianity, and, as we have said, in another place, this enmity still persists in many quarters.

The third method of the literal Qabalah is *Temurah.* This is a method of permutation, where one letter is substituted for another letter which either follows or precedes it in the alphabet, and an entirely different word is formed as a result. There are twenty-two sets of such letter permutations, including the most important one known as the "Qabalah of the Nine Chambers", but except for those who have devoted a very great amount of study to this method, it is of general interest only.

There is a second form of *Notaricon,* in which the initials of a sentence are taken to form a word or words. One of the most famous of such words is *Agla,* one of the Names of Power used in ceremonial magic, and having the meaning "Mighty art Thou, O Lord".

All these methods of the literal Qabalah are obviously akin to the methods of dream analysis used by psychologists today, and they provide a way by which many subconscious thought complexes may be brought into the waking consciousness. Herein lies their value. Also, because of the correlation of number and letter in the Hebrew alphabet, such artificial words and sentences are in the nature of formulae similar to the chemical formulae, which show, by their component letters, the elements from which certain compounds are built. Because of this, although this field of the literal Qabalah is full of traps for the unwary, it should be studied to some extent by the enquirer, in order that he may begin to understand something of the psychology which underlies the secret wisdom of the Hebrews.

The next division of our subject is the one which has made the greatest appeal to the ordinary public right down the ages. The practical Qabalah is that part of the Qabalistic work which deals with the magic of "woven paces and waving hands": Ceremonial and Talismanic Magic. Unfortunately this aspect of the Qabalah has become the heir to many of the most superstitious and degraded ideas and practices of both classical and medieval times, and has been chiefly studied from the baser motives of mankind. But beneath all the fraud and filth and folly of so many of its practitioners in times past, there lies a true and high doctrine and practice, which in the hands of those who are prepared to train and purify themselves, can be used for high spiritual purposes. In another chapter we shall deal more fully with this subject.

The last division of the Qabalah is what is known as "the unwritten Qabalah". This is a body of knowledge and practice which has been handed down from time immemorial, and is not in itself of Hebrew origin. The Qabalah has been used to act as a carrier for this deep esoteric teaching, but the teaching itself has been derived from many other sources. At various times men have claimed to have divulged the unwritten Qabalah, but, although teachings which have hitherto been reserved for the few *have* been made public, the true mysteries have not been betrayed — for the very good and sufficient reason that by their intrinsic nature they cannot be so divulged.

The true mysteries are experienced, not taught, and cannot be communicated to others by words. Only by inducing such a realization in those who are capable of being affected by it, can any communication of this arcane knowledge be attempted, and, even then, it is necessary that there should be some common language which may be used as a means whereby it may be discussed, and checked. The unwritten Qabalah uses the concepts and symbol-forms of the Qabalah as the alphabetical forms of a new language, and this new language can only be taught to those who are capable of receiving such "illuminations" as they are technically termed.

So the Mysteries are divided by a line of natural cleavage into the Lesser and the Greater Mysteries. In the Lesser Mysteries, information and teaching is given which can be understood by the reasoning mind, and the right use of this teaching will bring the aspirant to the point where it is possible for those who are his teachers to arouse in him a "realization" which will enable him to understand the language of the Greater Mysteries.

Because this is so, the Mysteries have been organized in a series of grades or steps, and in the Lesser Mysteries such grades can be taken irrespective of the moral or ethical standing of the person concerned. At the same time, however, they who bear rule therein usually see to it that unsuitable people are not automatically advanced because of their intellectual qualifications. Of course it does sometimes happen that such unsuitable ones do approach the Door of the Greater Mysteries, but by reason of their inability to *experience* the realities of that realm they are unable to proceed further and must perforce fall back.

To use a homely simile, a man may have spent much time in acquiring a full and detailed understanding of the principles of action of a motor cycle and of its parts; but, however much he may know of these things, if he attempts to ride that machine *before he has learnt to balance and control it,* he will be unable to do so. On the other hand, should he acquire the ability to ride it, he could get into serious trouble if he rode it without any knowledge of its parts and principles. To be a good motor-cyclist both knowledge and ability are necessary. This is also the case in the training and work of an initiate.

In the Lesser Mysteries he gains the basic information and begins to fit himself for the reception of those realizations which are the modes of experience in the Greater Mysteries.

If this were better understood by would-be apprentices to the Mysteries, they would save themselves much time and energy, and would be less liable to be deceived by unscrupulous "teachers" who arrogate to themselves lofty titles and pretensions.

It is to be noted that, although a man may attain to the grades of the Greater Mysteries, he cannot rest assured that he is safe from any retrogression. He holds his grade in those Mysteries by virtue of his functioning therein. As a tight-rope walker holds his position on the rope by a continued act of balancing, so the initiate holds his grade by effort and function. Only when he can worship "in the empty shrine" can he feel that he is relatively secure.

These Greater Mysteries, which are the core of the unwritten Qabalah are the centre around which all the Lesser Mystery Schools are organized. The initiates of these Greater Mysteries form a brotherhood known variously as "The Great White Lodge" or "The College of the Holy Spirit". It is dual in its work, dealing with the nations in accordance with their general cultural differences. So there is an Eastern Tradition, "they of the Ganges", and a Western Tradition, "they of the Andes". These two titles come from an old Rosicrucian source, for the true Order is one of the manifestations of the Western tradition.*

Also, although alchemy has had its followers in both East and West, it appeared in the West as a movement which had this same inspiration behind it.

In the latter half of the nineteenth century, a resurgence of the activities of the Western tradition brought into being new movements which, based on more ancient foundations, began to teach something of the ageless wisdom. Foremost among these was the movement known as "The Hermetic Order of Golden Dawn", and it is from this order that most of the Western esoteric movements stem.

At the same time, a corresponding impulse from the Eastern tradition had brought a new movement, "The Theosophical Society", to the attention of the world. This movement, by maintaining a public presentation of its teachings, has acted as a leaven which has affected much of that part of twentieth-century life which has been seeking, albeit unconsciously perhaps, for deeper teachings on life and destiny.

The original Order of the Golden Dawn foundered upon the rocks of personal jealousies and ambition, but the various split-off portions still survive and work with varying degrees of efficiency, and behind and through them work the masters of the Western tradition.

* Not to be identified with any advertising Fraternity.

# CHAPTER VII

# THE TREE OF LIFE

THE focal point around which the whole of the philosophy of the Qabalah is centred is the diagram or "mandala" known as the Tree of Life. In this chapter we will consider it purely as a diagram, reserving consideration of its component parts for later chapters.

The Tree consists of ten stations or *Sephiroth,* which are shown in a definite pattern. They are all connected by lines, twenty-two in number, and these ten circles and their connecting lines represent, in diagrammatic form, the Thirty-two Paths.

The general scheme of the Tree is that of a filing system, for it is held by the Qabalists that all manifestation can be classified under the ten headings of the *Sephiroth,* whilst the subjective reactions of all life and consciousness can be represented in the twenty-two connecting Paths.*

The Tree can be considered from several angles, and the first of these is its division into what are known as the Three Pillars. In certain organizations the Pillars of the Temple are said to be two, Jachin and Boaz, but the Qabalah teaches that there are three. It is held that whereas the two Pillars represent cosmic force and form respectively, the Middle Pillar deals with the element of consciousness in the manifest universe. It is taught that the inflowing energy of creation flows from a central point which is known as *Kether,* and thence to the *Sephiroth* of both the outer Pillars in an alternative path which is known as the Lightning Flash. The first station to which it proceeds is that termed *Chokmah,* and from thence it passes over the *Sephiroth Binah* which is at the head of the opposite Pillar of Form. It then crosses over again to the *Sephiroth Gedula,* or *Chesed,* as it is also called, back again to *Geburah,* or *Pachad* on the Pillar of Form. So the creative life proceeds until it finally manifests itself in the basic *Sephirah, Malkuth.*

Thus is the tree established in each of what are known as the Four Worlds. These are dealt with more fully elsewhere, and will only be mentioned briefly in this chapter.

Whilst this creative activity is taking place, the Middle Pillar is being established as the result of the balance attained between the two opposite pillars. Through this Middle Pillar manifests the emergent consciousness, the life-wave, for which the manifest universe, in all its aspects, visible and

---

* Though it is taught that certain other "Secret Paths" exist.

invisible, is the mighty stage upon which life plays its part. At the same time, the structure of this cosmic stage conditions and directs the play which is being produced upon it. In other words, life is not something apart from the universe, but an integral part of it. All manifestation is but the means whereby the life-wave, proceeding from the unmanifest, may in an emergent evolution become perfect in all its degrees.

So it is that the process of creation is symbolized by the glyph of the Tree, and the *Sephiroth* may be held to symbolize the points where the objective universe is held in manifestation, and the evolving life, as it emerges therefrom, partakes of all their qualities.

Wherever manifestation takes place, there is life coloured by the particular aspect of the universe in which that manifestation is taking place. So the relationship values symbolized in the Tree of Life are to be found also in every evolving consciousness. There is, therefore a microcosmic Tree within each human being, and between the personal consciousness and the universal self there is the same relationship as that which exists between the tidal waters of an almost landlocked bay and the ocean of which they are an integral part. So we recall that St Paul, quoting a Greek poet, says "For we are also His offspring"; and again, "In Him we live and move and have our being."

If we now turn to the lines which connect the ten *Sephiroth* with each other, we find that they represent the *modes of consciousness* both in the universe and the soul of man. When we are using the Tree in meditation work, we learn to tread these twenty-two paths in our inner consciousness, for it is in the region of consciousness that the application of the Tree takes place. The Qabalist (and we do not refer to the dry-as-dust pedant who has made the outer form of the Qabalah his field of study, but to the sincere follower of the tradition which has been handed down from one generation to another in the esoteric schools of the West) makes use of the Tree for the purposes of his own interior spiritual development.

To continue with our survey of the glyph as it is used in meditation work, it will be noted that each *Sephiroth* has a colour. Here we touch upon certain teachings into which we cannot go at the moment, but it is sufficient to say that the colour plan which runs throughout the whole of the Qabalistic scheme, is not there merely to give the Tree a festive appearance. It has a very definite part to play in any practical work upon it. There are four such colour scales, one for each of the Four Worlds of *Atziluth, Briah, Yetzirah* and *Assiah,* and it is usual to portray the Tree in one of these, usually as indicated in our diagram.

It will be seen that the *Sephirah Chokmah, Chesed,* and *Netzach* form one line or "pillar", whilst on the opposite side we find *Binah, Pachad* and *Hod,* forming the other pillar. The stations of *Kether, Daath, Tipareth,*

*Yesod* and *Malkuth* are located on the Middle Pillar. It will be noticed that in this last *Sephirah, Malkuth,* is the base of the entire Tree, and that it is linked up with all the other *Sephiroth.*

This is the furthest point of manifestation. The emerging consciousnesses who are playing their parts on the cosmic stage here turn from their outgoing activities and begin to return to their source. But whereas they emerged as a "life-wave", they return as individualized consciousnesses. It is the growth of individualized being which is the particular work that is being done in the material world, and for this reason this world is of the greatest importance. In the words of a great Qabalist, it is the marking-buoy of manifestation, and evolving human life must reach and pass round it before turning back on the return journey to the source from which it proceeded in the morning of manifestation.

Any attempt to by-pass the physical plane is foolish, for its lessons must be learnt, its battles essayed and its limitations accepted and used. Here we have again the same emphasis which recurs throughout the Qabalah: the importance of the physical world, and, because of that, the importance of the physical body which is our instrument for dealing with this world. The Qabalist, like the true Christian is enjoined to play his full part in the world, and not to attempt to flee from it. "Escapism" has never been the teaching of either Qabalism or Christianity, though throughout the years both systems of teaching have been contaminated by the erroneous doctrines of Manicheanism.

These doctrines regard the physical world and the physical body as evil in themselves, being the creations of an imperfect lesser god. The only way to salvation is, therefore, to repudiate all material things and attempt by ascetic living and by the practice of philosophy, to endeavour to return to the realms of light. There is a good deal of this kind of teaching to be found in the teachings of the Gnostics of early Christianity, and it is also present in the "doctrine of the two ways" which is found in two early Christian documents, the "Didache" and the "Epistle of Barnabas". But since Christianity developed in the matrix of Jewish thought, it took from it some of its basic ideas, and so we find this doctrine of the two ways in the manual of discipline of the Qumran Community on the shores of the Dead Sea, and even in the Old Testament itself; indeed, St Paul's remarks concerning the two laws he finds in himself have something of the same idea. This, as far as we can see, is chiefly due to the incorporation in both Jewish and Christian religious thought of certain Persian teachings.

It is easy to see that, for those who are for some reason or other pre-disposed to retreat from the world, this teaching holds great charm for it gives them chapter and verse for such retreat. However, from the point of view of the schools of esoteric Qabalism, it is an erroneous teaching.

Indeed, in its developed gnostic form it was repudiated by the church in the opening words of the Nicene Creed where God is described as the "Maker of heaven and earth and of *all things visible and invisible*".

If we have laboured this point it is because it is necessary to show how far this teaching is from the "woolly" and escapist philosophies of many modern esoteric schools, — but we are not claiming here that the teachings of the Qabalists have always been free from the dualistic heresy. The secret tradition has always been influenced by the temper of thought around it, and during certain periods, the Calvinistic ideas, which contain a large measure of dualism, have influenced what may be termed the top layers of the tradition; underneath the surface, however, the real teaching has remained unaffected by it.

Again, if we seem to have laboured the point of the extreme importance of the *Sephirah Malkuth,* it is in order that the very different attitude of many esoteric students towards the physical plane may be contrasted with the sane and balanced outlook of the Qabalistic teachings.

We now come to one of the most important aspects of the Tree of Life. There are two ways of storing goods. In one, everything is thrown indiscriminately into the store, and in the other each item is carefully packed and disposed of in such a way that it may the more easily be found when necessary. Most of the time, we follow method number one, and the only reason that our thoughts are not muddled far more than they are, is that the natural structure of the mind forces us to place them in some kind of order, just as the shape of our store-room would force us to dispose of the more bulky items of furniture in a certain way if we would get them in. So, as we have seen in a former chapter, the mind is built up in a very different pattern, and the best way in which we can store the knowledge we have gained is to pack it away in accordance with the mental architecture.

This the Tree of Life teaches us to do, since it conforms to that architecture very closely indeed. We may, therefore, now consider the Tree as a great "filing cabinet", by means of which we may sort out and store the knowledge we receive. We have, then a filing system of ten main headings: the ten *Sephiroth,* and a further twenty-two lesser ones: the interconnecting paths on the Tree.

For the time being we will concentrate on the primary headings of our system, and consider how they may be used. Each *Sephirah* has a certain primary "virtue" which is its keynote, and all persons, conditions and influences can be divided between one or other of these ten. But every good thing can be overdone in these lower worlds, and we find, therefore that the "vices" which are the unbalanced aspects of the virtues, also go to their own place: in this case to the ten stations of the *Qliphothic* Tree.

As an illustration let us take one *Sephirah,* and work it out in some detail.

Let us take *Chesed* on the right hand pillar of the Tree. Here we find the main heading which we must use is *Constructive Activity.* (The student is advised to make a card index system and to work on this classification.) Under this heading let us place on the appropriate index card the symbol of *Chesed.* This is a geometrical figure: the square. It should be coloured a clear blue, and if we have the necessary ability, we may place within the square a drawing of a majestic bearded king, seated on his throne. This gives the keynote of protective organization and preservation.

Now let us continue to use this method of classification. Looking around us, we find certain activities which come under the heading of protective control and preservation, and we therefore file these items under this head. For instance we may include the town and country planning authorities, wild-life preservation societies and so on — not forgetting the Civil Service. We often refer to these activities as "paternal" and this is also one aspect of *Chesed.* We may also profitably consider the building up processes of our physical bodies as coming under this heading. There will be people in our daily life who seem to portray this quality and we can file them accordingly. In this way we build up an organized complex of ideas all relating to one particular aspect of life.

This process is repeated with each *Sephirah* until there is built up an automatic subconscious habit of classification. It must be repeated here that the Qabalah is not only a system of philosophy, but that it is also, essentially, a method of using the mind in a certain way. The dry-as-dust pedant may occupy himself with the outer history or philosophic validity of the Qabalah, but the sincere student of esoteric tradition *uses* the system, and in the using obtains a far more balanced and objective view of the possibilities than the other.

One very important point in this respect is that no station on the Tree can ever be dealt with singly; always it is linked with all the others, and in particular with its opposite station; in the case of the *Sephiroth* on the two side pillars.

Thus, in the example we have just used, it is necessary that we now proceed to study the *Sephirah Pachad.* Here we have the concept of Severity, the geometric symbol in this case is a pentagon, within which we may place the image of a mighty warrior in his chariot. Here, in place of the beneficient organizing activities of *Chesed,* we have the violent disruption of existing conditions which so many people regard as the last evil. In truth this is not so, for the disintegrating activities of *Pachad* are the necessary balance to the organizing activities of *Chesed.*

We may again consider this in the same way that we have done with the other station. Let us imagine that we are going down the street on our way to work, and we catch sight of a row of buildings which are, we know, condemned as slums. We see that bulldozers and cranes are at work and the buildings are rapidly being demolished. This is an activity of *Geburah* or *Pachad*. There are those who would equate *good* with building up and organizing, and *evil* with breaking down and destroying, but it is clear that, in this present instance, the activities of Pachad are beneficent. There is a line in one of Tennyson's poems, King Arthur's dying speech, "The old order changeth, yielding place to new, and God fulfils Himself in many ways, *lest one good custom should corrupt the world.*"

The existence of the slum property is an example of the conserving activity of *Chesed* having become unbalanced, and the activity of *Pachad* is needed to break these conditions down and correct the balance.

But *Pachad* may also become unbalanced in the same way, and here we may again use a similar instance. On our daily walk to the station, we have seen that for some time a rather well-built house in obviously good condition has been empty. Now, as we pass it we see that hooligans, young and old, have begun to break down the fences, to smash the windows and to deface the building. Soon it will no longer be habitable, or even safe, for someone has been breaking down the walls themselves for purposes of their own. Here is an example of the unbalanced working of *Pachad*, and we would see, in the sudden irruption of council officials and building squads, the compensating activities of *Chesed*, making good the wanton destruction and so balancing the out-of-balance activities of *Pechad*.

If the Tree is used as a meditation system, then this is the kind of thing which must be done with each of the *Sephiroth* in turn. It is important to remember that the opposed *Sephiroth* together form a working unit, and it is this unit which must be dealt with in all practical work upon the Tree. Thus we have certain "functional triangles" as they are termed. The first of these is known as the Supernal Triangle, and is made up of the *Sephiroth Kether, Chokmah* and *Binah*. This is the root and basis upon which all manifestation is grounded, and between it and the rest of the *Sephiroth* there is a gulf fixed, known as the "abyss". This means that all subsequent manifestation is of a different quality to these three, and to understand the supernals fully an entire change of consciousness is necessary. These three, the source which is *Kether*, the father which is *Chokmah* and the mother which is *Binah*, are the governing factors for the rest of the Tree. The station *Chokmah* is regarded as the positive masculine potency of manifestation, and the station, *Binah,* as the passive feminine potency thereof. As will be seen from the diagram, these three supernals stand at the head of each of the three pillars of the Tree.

Now here we come to the mysterious station known as *Daath*. This seems to have no connection with the rest of the Tree, and is apparently an eleventh station, yet the Qabalistic texts are emphatic that there are only ten *Sephiroth*. Herein lies a mystery, but it may be suggested that *Daath* has to do with dimensions of consciousness. There is a Qabalistic saying that *Kether* is the *Malkuth* of the unmanifest, that is, that in each of the Four Worlds, the last phase of manifestation of each world is the source and beginning of the next.

We may then conceive of *Daath* as being, amongst other things, the connecting link of *consciousness* between the Worlds. Thus, *Daath* in *Atziluth* links directly with *Daath* in *Briah*, and that with *Daath* in *Yetzirah* until the world of *Assiah* is reached. This linking station in all the worlds would appear to be the apex of a pyramid whose base is made up of *Kether*, *Chokmah* and *Binah*, and this apex exists or subsists in another dimension.

The next triangle is that of *Pachad* and *Chesed* which finds its point in *Tiphareth*, and the third is that composed of *Netzach*, *Hod* and *Yesod*.

The tenth *Sephirah*, *Malkuth* is the point where all the influences of the Tree are received and dealt with, and the evolving lives in the manifested universe begin their return to the source from which they came.

It will be seen that the Middle Pillar contains the stations which are the equilibrated energies of the two outer pillars, and any consideration of either of these must take into account not only the polarizing opposite of the station concerned, but also the equilibrating third station of that functional triangle.

In fact, whenever we are dealing with the Tree, either as a meditation symbol or as a general diagram of the disposition of manifest things, we are always to remember that the Tree must, in the last resort, be considered as a whole, even though we may be concentrating upon some particular aspect of it at a given time.

# CHAPTER VIII

# THE FOUR WORLDS OF THE QABALISTS

THE philosophy of the Qabalists is an "emanation" philosophy, and here it comes into direct opposition to the ideas of orthodox Christianity. This opposition is, however, based upon certain misconceptions and is in point of fact gradually changing under the impact of modern knowledge. The old idea of the Eternal as the personal artificer in creation is changing as the immensities of creation are unveiled.

In the last analysis, of course, it is very true to say that God created all things, but the way in which this was done, as set forth by the Qabalah, is different to the ideas of exoteric Judaism which have been taken over into orthodox Christianity. The great objection of Christian theologians to the emanationist philosophy is that it tends towards pantheism, which can be equated so easily with the idea that "God" is simply the totality of Nature. But this the Qabalah does not teach. Quite rightly it teaches that God is made manifest in Nature, and is immanent in it: but it also teaches that all manifestation, on whatever plane, is only one expression of the eternal being who reigns transcendent over all. It should be noted here that in this philosophy there is no rigid dichotomy; no hard and fast division between Spirit and Matter. Matter is regarded as "the luminous garment of the Eternal", indeed as being an expression of that Being, and therefore all things are holy in their intrinsic nature. This idea, as will be seen, cuts right across the Manichaean strain which still persists in some parts of Christianity, one of its manifestations being what is commonly known as puritanism.

Assuming that the emanationist philosophy is correct how then is creation effected? Here we come to the idea of the "agents" through whom creation takes place, and also to the modes of that creation. It must be clearly understood that these realms of creation which are called "worlds", are not spacial planets or anything of that kind. We say this because even those who should have known better have sometimes fallen into this error. Let us then define what is meant by the term. *A "world" in this connection refers to a particular mode of activity of the Deity.*

The first of these modes is known as the world of *Atziluth,* or the archetypal world. It is the field of the divine ideas which are behind all manifestation. Here the divine mind manifests those abstract concepts which will later be worked out in increasing complexity in all the fields of manifestation. The glyph of the Tree of Life is held by the Qabalists to be established in all the "worlds" and here it is understood to be present in its most refined form. It is a spiritual "blue-print" in the divine mind. This is not to say that the figure which we draw and describe as the Tree is present in the world of *Atziluth as a figure,* but rather that the *relationships* figured in the Tree have here their origins.

We come next to the world of *Briah.* In the Qabalah this world of *Briah* is also called the World of Thrones and is held to emanate from the world of *Atziluth.* It is, as it were, a step nearer to the objectivity of matter, and is sometimes known as the Creative World, since it is here that the archetypes of the *Atziluthic* World begin to be objectified, and it is here that the "archangels" are held to be actively engaged in formulating the divine archetypes. It is a "world" in which the primal energy of manifestation begins its work.

It is to be understood that the "archangels" are not in any way to be thought of as superhuman beings having a human form and possessing wings such as popular piety would have us believe. The same may also be said of the angelic and subhuman orders of life.

The third world is the world of *Yetzirah,* the world of formation. Here the substance of manifestation is still without any *material* expression, and it is here that those beings known as the angels have their true abode. Here the universe builders are, as it were, making their arrangements for the materialization of the divine archetypes in physical expression, and this physical expression takes place in the fourth world, that of *Assiah.*

*Assiah* is said to be made up of the grosser elements of the preceding three worlds. By this we understand that there is a gradation of complexity of substance in these worlds (which, it must be kept in mind, are non-material), and this gradation results in a similar gradation of material physical matter. As we shall see, the Tree of Life is implicit in all the four worlds, and the relationships it portrays show a similar gradation. Since, as we have said, all the four worlds are interpenetrating "states", the finer and grosser aspects of them all are to be found in the last world to be emanated, and the grossest of them all is the *Sephirah* at the foot of the Tree of Life, the *Sephirah* known as *Malkuth.*

It is here, in the world of *Assiah,* that we come to another Qabalistic concept which is of real importance. Below *Assiah* is said to be formulated the kingdom of the *Qliphoth.* Briefly, it may be said that the *Qliphoth* are the unbalanced aspects of the Tree of Life formulated in the waters of chaos in an averse Tree of ten stations. Thus there appears an infernal Tree of ten stations, corresponding to the ten Holy *Sephiroth.*

The origin of this realm of the *Qliphoth* is to be found in the processes of manifestation by which the universe came into being. This was begun by the outpouring of the primal power from the unmanifest through the

*Sephirah Kether,* and this power in turn expressed itself through the other *Sephiroth* until *Malkuth* was reached. But, as we have already pointed out, the essence of the Tree is *balance,* and in the beginning of the outpouring of Cosmic Life through each *Sephirah* there is no balance; not until the corresponding station is emanated does such a balance become possible. It follows, then, that during the establishment of each *Sephirah* there is an overplus of differentiated energy, and this goes into what may be termed "the waters under the earth". Thus there exists in the universe this realm of unbalanced force; the realm of "the Kings of Edom, who reigned before there was a King in Israel". Now, all manifested life has been, and still is to a very great extent indeed, out of harmony, at least here in *Malkuth* of *Assiah,* and this unbalance means that there are built up organized centres of unbalance in the chaotic world of unorganized energy which is the kingdom of the *Qliphoth,* and as the positive evil of the world is an expression of the unbalance of the doers of evil, so each disharmony goes to its own place, linking up with that aspect of the *Qliphoth* which is of its own nature. Thus, in the course of the ages, are built up the mighty unbalanced complexes of positive evil, complexes which are energized by the terrible energies of the waters under the earth.

It is possible to obtain power in three ways. The first way is that of approach to the fountain-head of all power and the endeavour to become a channel of that power; the second way is, as it were, an attempt to "rob Peter to pay Paul" by juggling with the energies of manifestation; and the third way is that of reversion to the waters of chaos, and of becoming the channel through which the unbalanced power of that kingdom may emerge in terrible action.

In the terms of Jungian psychology, we may regard the *Qliphoth* as the unbalanced aspects of the archetypes of the collective unconsciousness of the race. Always there is a pressure from the waters under the earth, and this pressure will find release through any channel which is open to it. So the fanatical dictator, whether of the right or the left finds himself buoyed up by some apparently irresistible power, and everything seems possible to him. However, as the *Qliphothic* energies begin to flow through him in an increasing stream, he finds that they are beginning to take control. No longer can he exert the authority which was his and direct his activities in accordance with reason. The energies are commencing to become inner dictators and to drive him whither, in his reasonable moments, he would not wish to go. Now he begins to make mistakes, his strategy becomes faulty, and the unbalanced forces which he has released in those who blindly follow him, now begin to work upon them in such a way as to bring about disloyalty and disruption within the nation. Finally, the whole system of dictatorial power crumbles, and his reign is over.

It is held by one school of esoteric training that, when Christ hung on the Cross, it was not in the agony of death by crucifixion, there are more terrible forms of torture, but in the taking unto Himself the accumulated unbalanced force and abreacting it, that His real work was accomplished. Then, by a stupendous alchemy He transmuted it into unbalanced power, available for the helping of the world, and, whilst a great change was affected in the psychic atmosphere of this planet, a new and living way was opened up through which man could approach the eternal.

We have been speaking of "positive evil", and this may perhaps need some explanation. In this system of thought evil is not regarded in quite the same way as it is in popular thought. It is held that there is, what is termed "negative evil", and this is simply the reaction to the energies of the creative logos. Friction, which engineers and motorists attempt to keep as low as possible when they apply it to their machinery, is nevertheless one of the most important factors in its operation. If a road surface were entirely without frictional qualities, if such a thing were possible, the energy of the motor would make the wheels go round, but they would not be able to get any purchase on the road and would spin uselessly. Any motorist who has had to get his car out of a snowdrift or out of a piece of marshy land will appreciate this, as will, also, any skater who, at the beginning of his career, appreciated the truth of the saying that skates should be sold in sets of three! Thus negative evil is regarded as the necessary reaction to the application of the creative forces, without which any creation would be impossible.

This brings us back to the opening statement of the *Book of the Concealed Mystery. The Book of the Concealed Mystery* is "the book of the equilibrium of balance". As the *Sephiroth* are established in each "world", they appear in balanced form, one pulling against the other, as it were, in order to achieve the equilibrium which is the ideal of manifestation. Here we have the source of what is known as "dualism", for if we think only of the opposition of the *Sephiroth,* we shall tend to regard some of them as "evil", but if we regard this "push-pull" as the establishment of a dynamic balance, we shall see that the apparent antagonism is illusory, and that it springs from a mistaken view of manifestation. However, during the period in which this dynamic balance is being established, there will be unbalanced power at large in the universe, and this will, as we have said, gravitate to its appropriate centre in the regions of the *Qliphoth:* the "Habitations of Hell", as they are sometimes termed.

If we regard the whole process of manifestation as being a mighty flow of power from a creative centre, and its ultimate return thereto, then we may think of negative evil as being the resistance of the field of manifestation to the organizing principle in that emanation of power, the friction and opposition which enables that principle to formulate therein. This, then, is part of the mechanism of creation, and is necessary in order that manifestation may take place. There will also be that opposition which is due to the fact that pressure of creation in one direction has not fully ceased before a new phase of activity begins to take place, and thus the initial activity of the new phase is impeded in its beginnings. But all this is comprehended within the cosmic scheme.

What is not included in the cosmic scheme is what we have termed "positive evil", that is to say, it has no intrinsic function to perform therein, as is the case with negative evil. Rather is it a failure arising from the unbalanced actions of the life-units of the scheme, for implicit in the whole universe (and, according to the Qabalists, in the whole of creation), is the principle of "free will", and it is here that positive evil has its roots. Thus the freewill of the units of life tends to organize the unbalanced forces for its own purpose; in this way organized positive evil becomes a foreign body of the Heavenly Man (as the whole field of manifestation is termed by the Qabalists) and two courses are possible in order to deal with this positive evil, just as in the physical body an effort is made to absorb or reject a foreign substance: so in Macroprosopos a similar effort is made. Where it is possible, the positive organized energy of positive evil is absorbed into the general circulation of power in the universe by a process which is equivalent to the "abreaction" used in modern psychiatrical treatment. This process, which must always take place in and through the densest level of manifestation if it is to be effective, works through the developed and dedicated beings who find in this work their natural line of action, and throughout the ages of evolution such cosmic abreaction has been effected by them. According to certain Qabalists the outflowing stream of manifestation reached its lowest point on the physical level some two thousand years ago, and at this point it should have been possible for the Logos of Light so to enter into the evolving life, that henceforth it would have been possible for it to evolve to its perfection and return to its source in a balanced and orderly manner. However, the power of positive evil was such that, despite the efforts of previous dedicated beings, there was a danger that the whole scheme might be temporarily "bogged down" and retarded in such a way that the whole of evolving life would fail to turn the corner, and, passing beyond the point of return for aeonian time, cause the entire cosmic scheme to be thrown out of balance.

So the incarnation of the Logos had to be devoted to the restoration of the balance, and this He did by drawing to himself the unbalanced forces, and, by a supreme alchemy, transmuting them in such a way that the evolving life was able to pass the nadir and begin, *en masse,* to tread the path of return. That which before was limited to the few became an opportunity for the many, for He opened up a new and living way whereby mankind might be able to surge ahead towards the spritual home, and, not only mankind alone, for by His cleansing of the psychic sphere of the planet, all the lives thereon, subhuman and elemental alike shared in this liberation.

This also was the belief of the early Christian church before the legalistic Roman mind began to formulate the Christian Good News in legal terms. It was held quite simply that Christ had fought and conquered the powers of evil, and released the whole cosmic order from its bondage to the Lords of Unbalanced Force, so that all might now be able to return safely home to the eternal. This view of the atonement is one which can be held by anyone, for *no official definition of the Atonement has been formulated by any of the great councils of the Catholic Church.*

This whole question of the Atonement is ably worked out in Aulen's *Christus Victor.* It is mentioned here in order to show how the Qabalistic concepts were used and still are, by Christian Qabalists.

It may seem that this consideration of the *Qliphoth* has little to do with the Four Worlds, but it is because it concerns them by virtue of the fact that, on every one of them, with the exception of the world of *Atziluth,* the shadowy waters under the Earth are to be found. The archangel of *Briah* has his counterpart in the Devil in the Habitations of Hell, and the angels their counterpart in the demons of the Habitations.

Now the unbalanced forces in the worlds of *Briah* and *Yetzirah* were passive and unorganized, but with the evolution of consciousness and self-consciousness in the world of *Assiah,* they began to be organized into a force of positive evil, warring against the light, and so the Habitations of Hell came into existence.

Though the victory over the powers of evil has been won on aeonian levels, man has still to apply that victory in his own personal realm, and to "fight manfully against the world the flesh and the devil", as the Anglican Catechism puts it. This warfare must be fought in the dust and turmoil of everyday life. This world is the battlefield of *Kurukshetra,* as the great Hindu epic of the Gita terms it.

Here the teachings of the Qabalah can be usefully applied, and although in some cases battles may be won by retreating, after the manner of Fabius Cunctator, yet for the great bulk of humanity it is here, on the physical plane, in the grind of mundane life, that the victory must be gained. It is because of this that the Qabalists lay such great stress upon the station of *Malkuth* in *Assiah,* and it is also the reason why we have devoted this space to the consideration of the *Qliphoth,* for it is here in the world of matter that they must be met and overcome.

# CHAPTER IX

## CONCERNING ADAM KADMON

IN several ancient philosophies the eternal source of all manifestation is imaged under the form of a great Man. This idea, in the hands of the primitive type of mind produces what has been termed "anthropomorphism", and this has been a fruitful source of trouble in most of the religious systems of the world.

For it is quite justifiable to think of God in some kind of earth imagery — in fact it is almost impossible to do otherwise. Even the strictest monotheist and metaphysician must use *some* earth terms if he is to convey anything to his followers, and though, following Eastern precedent he may attempt to define the Eternal by using negative terms *Neti, neti* "Not this, not that", nevertheless he cannot avoid the employment of positive terms, even though he uses them in a negative way.

Thus, if he says, "God is Love, He is more than that, for our earthly concept of love is only the shadow of a shadow of the reality," he has had to use the positive term, and to some extent define it in order to express the idea which he is trying to convey.

We have said that the anthropomorphic tendency has caused much trouble in the religious world. This is because the multitudes usually employ a subconscious mental mechanism known as "projection". This means that we tend to give to an outer image the emotions and instinctive values which are in ourselves. This projection takes place in varying degrees, but very few people entirely escape its employment. This mechanism, when it is employed in religious work, can give rise to some very queer ideas as to the nature of the Supreme Being. I think it was Dean Swift who remarked on one occasion that God made man in His own Image, and man had replied by making God in *his* image, "complete with shovel hat". This is true of the majority of people. A man with a strong streak of cruelty in his nature will conceive of God as a great figure of terror ruling over the affairs of men, and he will find in the sacred scriptures of his religion "proof-texts" which, when wrenched from their context will justify him in thinking of the Supreme in this way. What is more, and this is the most important point, he will be able to justify his own use of cruelty to others by pointing to similar action by the God he worships.

Some of the worst excesses of the Christian churches throughout the centuries have been condoned and "justified" by such use of the Old

Testament, and this is not peculiar to Christianity. All religious movements have been affected by it, for projection is not something which is purely western and Christian; it is a psychological mechanism common to the whole of humanity.

The genius of the Qabalah has been to take this universal tendency and turn it to service by boldly using anthropomorphic images, but using them in a certain definite way, so that instead of being a source of trouble, they will help the mind to reach up to concepts which seem to lie far beyond the mental horizon.

It may be noted in passing, that the idea of the Heavenly Man is not peculiar to the Qabalists. It is to be found in the Hindu esoteric teachings, and reappeared in the West in the teachings and revelations of the great Swedish seer Swedenborg. In his teaching every form of life has its appropriate place in the body of the Heavenly Man, and this too, is to be found in another guise in the teachings of the Western tradition.

The Heavenly Man of the Qabalah is held to be the manifestation of what is termed *Arik Anpin,* the Great Countenance, which is the *Sephirah Kether* expanded in *Chokmah* and *Binah.* Now these three are the three supernals between whom and the rest of the Tree is placed the abyss to signify that they differ from the others in a special way. *Chokmah,* which is the positive, male principle, and *Binah* the negative female principle unite in *Daath,* or to put it in another way, the equilibrium of these two enable the emerging consciousness to begin to manifest in the other *Sephiroth.* The root of *Arik Anpin,* or Macroposopos is to be found in *Kether,* just as the root of the Heavenly Man, Microposopos, is to be found in *Tiphareth.*

The Microposopos is also known as *Zaur Anpin,* or the Lesser Countenance, and is made up of *Chesed, Pachad, Netzach, Hod* and *Yesod,* centred in Tiphareth. It will be seen that this leaves out the *Sephirah Malkuth.* This *Sephirah* is sometimes called "The Bride of Microposopos", or else *Kellah,* the queen, in which case Microposopos is known as the king.

It is also said that *Malkuth* "is exalted above every head, and sits upon the throne of *Binah*". Now *Binah* is also termed the Superior Mother, and *Malkuth* therefore becomes the Inferior Mother.

In the *Greater Holy Assembly,* one of the books of the *Zohar,* Rabbi Schimeon is stated to have said to his co-workers "Now take your places to describe how the parts of Microposopos are confirmed . . . from the forms of the Ancient of Days, the Holy of the Holy Ones, the Withdrawn of the Withdrawn Ones, the Concealed One of All. But the conformations of Microposopos are disposed from the forms of Macroposopos; — and His constituent parts are expanded on this side and on that, *under a human form,* so that there may be manifest in Him the Spirit of the Concealed One in every part."

We may interpret this as a declaration that the Heavenly Man is the field in which all manifestation takes place, and He is also the Pleroma or fullness of all the powers, forces and forms to be found therein, whilst His consciousness is the root and ground of all consciousness in creation. This is the Cosmic Christ of modern esoteric thought, and in Him we truly live and move and have our being.

In this mighty figure of the Heavenly Man, the Qabalah is placing before us the concept of a living universe, in contradistinction to the arid lifeless concept of modern materialistic science, or, to be more accurate, of that section of science which still thinks in terms of the Victorian period. For many scientists are nowadays beginning to visualize all manifestation as the working of a mighty consciousness.

Again, a word of warning is necessary. The great glyph of the Heavenly Man is valuable as indicating an actual series of relationships between the various factors in the universe, but it is these *relationships* which are of the essence of the matter. It is so easy to use the glyph as a substitute for the reality it expresses.

There is yet another doctrine of the Heavenly Man which claims attention. There is a teaching that there exist certain men who have, through repeated incarnations, attained perfection *within this planetary system.* They are variously known as the brothers, the masters, the holy ones, the mahatmas, according to the various schools of West and East. It is held that each of these masters represents the perfection of one type of consciousness, and is, as it were, the centre around which the evolving consciousness of men group themselves, each according to his type of "ray".

So, in each cycle of cosmic history, there is built up a Heavenly Man after the manner of the Swedenborgian revelations, each evolving consciousness gravitating to that position in the Heavenly Man which is the position for his type. At the same time all the lives are interdependent and form one consciousness; as emergent evolution proceeds, so all lives begin to become conscious of position in the cosmic scheme, a position which they have always held, but of which they were not aware. So Microposopos becomes realized in the reciprocal Heavenly Man which is evolved. This process is repeated, so says the tradition, through seven great epochs of evolution, until at the end there is to be found one Heavenly Man which consciously mirrors the mind and consciousness of the Eternal, that mind and consciousness which is immanent in all manifestation, and which in the Qabalah is known as Adam Kadmon.

All of this may be expressed in the symbols used by a modern writer, and with them we may profitably conclude this chapter.

". . . there appeared in the Rose of Light, at the diamond point where being enters into manifestation, the perfect form of a Man; androgyne, if the expression may be allowed, at which the whole concourse of adorants swept to their knees, Thrones, Powers, Dominions themselves, for in all Heaven there is no Power that is not a form of the Light, and Beyond Light, and no Power has power that does not know this."

"I remember . . . we all have in ourselves the power of cognition by symbol, which next to silence is most eloquent; and I have not forgotten the symbol which Venus held out, the symbol which speaks with power in all worlds. We were to see it again . . . the Cross on which, if I may so express myself, Light dies; the Rose, if I may venture, in which Light is born."*

*A Visit from Venus, p. 155. Also Trout's Testament, p. 179. Both books by Sir Ronald Fraser. Published by Jonathan Cape.

# CHAPTER X

## CONCERNING THE VEILS

WHEN we study the glyph of the Tree of Life we find that the first *Sephirah, Kether,* appears to have a background shown as three concentric arcs and named *Ain, Ain Soph* and *Ain Soph Aur* respectively. If *Kether* is the source of all manifestation what then are these Veils, as they are termed?

The answer is that they are the symbols of the unmanifest, from which *Kether* proceeds. For, of course, all manifestation must have some root in that which, in itself is unmanifest. The philosopher Herbert Spencer regarded this as not only The Unknown, but as The Unknowable; this is true, of course, if we regard the mind as a finished product. But, as evolution of both life and consciousness proceeds, many things which once were unknowable, become knowable for the instrument we are using is becoming more efficient.

At the same time it must be remembered that, although the instrument may be more efficient, this will not avail unless a development also takes place in the consciousness. This latter is not merely a quantitative advancement; it also concerns the unfolding of a new quality.

Dion Fortune likens the use of the veils in practical esotericism to the employment of algebraic symbols in the calculations of the higher mathematics. In themselves the symbols are meaningless, but they enable the mind to deal with problems which would otherwise be impossible of solution. So with the whole of the inter-related symbolism of the Tree of Life; it is a system of mathematics dealing with cosmic unknowns.

But, it may be asked, why should these highly abstruse ideas be considered; why not leave them in a decent obscurity, and get on with the practical side of esotericism?

There are several reasons for the establishment of the symbolic veils in the student's mind, and the most important of these is that it roots all esoteric work in a source which cannot in any way be used as a mental finality. Whenever the esotericist is dealing with any manifested appearance, he must always regard it against the background of the veils, and in this way he is taught to avoid the establishment of a mental fixed point. Always beyond lies the unmanifest, and it is against this background that all his life and work is set.

Another use of the veils is to express in symbolic terms the fact that manifestation is not only a "being", but also that it is a "becoming". So the

Name of God, which is given to *Kether,* is *Ehieh Asher Ehieh,* translated
in our Bible as "I am that I am". A friend of the writer, a notable Qabalist,
suggests that a better translation would be "I am the Ever-becoming One".
Here we have the idea of an outflowing form, the unmanifest, this resulting
in all manifestation. So, in this name of the Eternal, we are given the
concept of a rhythmic unfoldment of the activity of God, with no absolute
finality: always a becoming, never an absolute ending. Many followers of
the orthodox religions, both Christian and non-Christian, would dissent
from this idea, but this is, in the main, due to the normal desire for
completion of work and "refreshment after labour". That there is such a
satisfying completion of the evolutionary journey of the spirit of man is
true, but this philosophy teaches that the completion of one phase of
manifestation is followed, after a period of bliss and happiness beyond
earthly imagining, by a fresh adventure of the spirit, as the activity of the
ever-becoming One again opens out the starry ways. So, again and again,
the divine life surges into manifestation; again and again it "rests from its
labours" and withdraws itself into the fruits of its activity; and again and
again, in new aspects of its fathomless being, are conceived new and
exciting adventures of manifestation.

Here we have the Qabalistic equivalent of what is known in the East as
the cycle of the "Days and Nights of Brahma". In the East, it is true that
this divine activity is thought of, more or less entirely, as the working out
of inevitable law, but in the schools of the Western tradition such a concept
is associated with the idea of the working-out, by a supreme artist, of a
vision of beauty which is part of its nature. So, aeon after aeon the plans
of God are worked out, the cosmic picture is completed, and the Artist
rests; whilst all the beings who have been the actors upon His stage, parts
of His cosmic masterpiece, enter into the "joy of the Lord", until, after
what in temporal terms are untold ages, once more the divine fiat goes
forth, and the sons and daughters of God shout aloud for joy in that fair
morning of a new creation. So from eternity unto eternity the ever-
becoming One expresses Himself, and all this is symbolized by the veils.

Now since the veils portray "negative existence", any earthly image we
may make of them is, of course, entirely misleading. We cannot predicate
of "that which is" anything which can be expressed in earth terms. This
is taught both in Eastern philosophies and in Christian theology. *'Neti,
neti,* Not this, not that," says the Eastern sage, and the mystical theology
of the pseudo-Dionysius, and the mysterious author of that wonderful
treatise *The Cloud of Unknowing,* say the same thing.

But although we cannot give "a local habitation and a name" to the
underlying realities symbolized by the veils, we can use the veils as a
background against which we may judge all manifestation, or that part of

it which we are able to understand at any given time. For the mind of man, as it grows, becomes able to understand more and more of manifestation, and so the veils recede as man progresses.

It is evident, therefore, that some set these veils in one position, whilst others go far beyond their fellows, and penetrate deeply into the mystery. But although we may, in this way, suggest the idea of "negative existence", we must be careful not to *define* it too closely. For whatever we define comes within the compass of our mind, and therefore ceases to be infinite. Only when we have experienced in our spiritual self something of that infinity can we be said to comprehend it.

"If God can be understood, then He is no longer God," said one philosopher, and this simply means that the use of the rational faculty cannot, *of itself*, define the infinite. But by a mystical comprehension, we may understand something of that which is the root and foundation of all.

Fawcett, in one of his books* goes into this matter in some detail, and although we would not agree with all his conclusions, we would strongly recommend his writings to those who find metaphysics a congenial field of study.

We have, therefore, two modes or ideas, negative and positive existence, which in themselves are irreconcilable, and here the graded symbol of the veils helps us. McGregor Mathers, in *The Kabbalah Unveiled,* says, "between these two ideas, a certain connecting link is required, and hence we arrive at the form which is called *potential existence,* which, while more nearly approaching positive existence, will still scarcely admit of clear definition. It is existence in its *possible* form. For example, in a seed, the tree which may spring forth from it is hidden: it is in a condition of potential existence; it is there; but it will not admit of definition. How much less, then, will those seeds which that tree in its turn may yield be defined, for these latter are in a condition which, while it is somewhat analogous to potential existence, is at a stage even less advanced, that is, they are negatively existent. On the other hand, positive existence is always capable of definition; it is dynamic; it has certain evident powers, and it is therefore the antithesis of negative existence. It is the tree, no longer hidden in the seed, but outwardly developed and manifested."

Positive existence has a beginning and an end, and it therefore requires another form from which to depend, for without this other concealed negative ideal behind it, it is unstable and unsatisfactory.

Thus, then, have I faintly and with all reverence, endeavoured to foreshadow in the minds of my readers, the idea of the Illimitable One; and before that idea, and of that idea, I can only say, in the words of an

* *Divine Imagining,* Douglas Fawcett (MacMillan & Co., London, 1921).

ancient oracle, "In Him is an illimitable abyss of glory, and from it there goeth forth one little spark which maketh all the glory of the sun and of the moon and of the stars. Mortal! behold how little I know of God; seek not to know more of Him, for this is far beyond thy comprehension, however wise thou art; as for us, who are His ministers, how small a part we are of Him!"

There is yet another "veil" in Qabalistic philosophy. It is termed *Paroketh,* and is drawn across the diagram of the Tree of Life through the *Sephirah Tiphareth.* Beyond this veil *Paroketh* there lies the *abyss* as it is named — the level of consciousness and manifestation which is of an entirely different quality to the lower personal self.

There is a tendency, common to many aspirants to esoteric knowledge, to attempt to soar in the rarified air of abstract ideas to the neglect of what are erroneously thought to be inferior states and conditions of being. Veil *Paroketh* is intended to warn the Qabalist that he must not lose himself in a labyrinth of abstract speculation, but work within the present limits of his mental capacity. By so doing he avoids becoming "woolly-minded", and, this very limitation of thought will develop his consciousness to the point where he can effect that change of consciousness which will take him across the abyss into an entirely new world of being. He has then become reborn in eternity, to use a phrase which was used in the old mystery schools.

But until he has so developed, it is a wise policy for him to concentrate upon the levels of the Tree which lie below *Tiphareth.* He must "tarry in Jerusalem until his beard is grown".

This device of the veil *Paroketh* may be applied to the study of every part of the Tree. It is a very useful method of limiting the field of mental vision and endeavour, and corresponds, in the mental field, to the artist's device of screening off the area of vision by his hands, so that he sees only a part of the total scene, but sees that with greater clarity.

Here it is as well to remember that there is yet another check on the tendency to soar in mental pride. It is said in this philosophy "A Tree in every *Sephirah*". We live on the planet Earth, and we have a consciousness which has been furnished with earth images and concepts. Within this sphere of Earth, *Malkuth* on the Tree, we must realize that there is the reflection of that, which in its true nature, lies far beyond. "As above, so below" runs the Hermetic axiom. So all the aspects of the Tree are present in *Malkuth,* and it is on this level that we must first contact them. So always we must remember that when we begin to have mystical and occult experience, we are working within the rainbow aura of Earth; we are contacting *Tiphareth* or *Binah* or *Kether under the veil of earthly things.*

# CHAPTER XI

# THE NEW OCCULTISM

I HAVE tried in this book to give some idea of the nature of modern esoteric lore, and to indicate some of its sources. I have purposely written in a way which will probably irritate some of my readers. I am sorry if this is the case, but I have written not only to instruct but to affect the deeper levels of the mind; this has meant that the subject matter has been presented in what may appear to be an irrational way. Those who, having read this book, use its chapters as food for meditation practice will find therein something which will, I believe, be helpful in the work of producing those changes in consciousness which are the goals of magical art.

"Of the making of books there is no end," and certainly there have been many published works which deal with the secret wisdom of Israel, the Qabalah, and with the esoteric schools which derive their power and inspiration from that particular presentation of the ageless wisdom. Unfortunately, so much of what has been published by one person, or group of persons, appears to be but a rehash of what someone else has already written. To some extent this must be true. We build upon the foundations laid by others, and our own work, if valid, serves in its turn as the level from which others build. What is new in our work, is not the scheme which we outline, but rather that particular form in which we present it. It is here that the unique contribution of any new writer lies, and it is here that the growing point of esoteric science is to be found. Most of the published material dealing with the Western Esoteric Tradition has been drawn from the rituals and knowledge papers of the Hermetic Order of the Golden Dawn as they were revealed by Aleister Crowley, Dr Israel Regardie and other members of that order, or of similar Orders, such as *Argentum Astris* and *Stella Matutina*. The rituals once revealed lose their power, although they can be used as subjects for meditation and can, under these circumstances, be of very great help to the earnest student.

It may be as well if I indicate, at this point, what is my own position in this matter. In my early days I was fortunate in making contact with one who taught with authority in this field, and my debt to this man (known to his students as "R.K.") is very great indeed. Later, in the East, I came into contact with a group of Indian occultists, and by a most curious concatenation of circumstances, I found, on my return to this country, another teacher, the late "Dion Fortune", and I made my esoteric home in the Fraternity she founded. Dion Fortune was at first a member of the Order of the Golden Dawn, under *Mrs* McGregor Mathers, and later transferred to the Order Stella Matutina. Because of this, her general outlook was that of the G.D.

An extensive contact with psychic and occult matters through my work with my first teacher, together with a great deal of independent personal experience in the psychic and occult fields, enabled me to make use of the material given me in the Fraternity in a distinct way. Based upon my own personal psychism, plus the body of teaching received from these several sources, my books have been written to help others to attain to some of the glimpses of reality which it has been my good fortune to have received myself.

In the new age which we are now entering, revolutionary changes are taking place, and the esoteric schools must, to some extent at least, adjust themselves to the new tempo of life if they are to be of service to humanity. It has to be recognized that, like many other venerable institutions, the esoteric fraternities have accumulated much unnecessary lumber in their passage through the centuries. Some of this lumber is to be found embedded in the rituals of the Fraternities (like the fossil in the rock), and it has a certain secondary value, since it links the present-day consciousness with the primitive levels of the archetypes in the collective unconscious of the race. However, there is much which could be jettisoned with advantage, and those who rule in the lodges must needs grasp this nettle if they are to deal effectively with the people and conditions of the changing world.

Bread and wine and a validly ordained priest are all that are necessary to the offering of the Catholic Oblation. In a similar way, the essentials of esoteric science are far fewer than many would have us realize. It should not be forgotten that just as Our Lord likened the Kingdom of Heaven to a wise householder who brings forth from his treasures things *old and new*, so must the esoteric schools achieve balance in this new age by developing a new approach. This must be done by building upon the true foundations which were shown them in olden times "in the mount", a structure which may be integrated into the life and work of today.

With one such endeavour I am myself associated, and it remains to be seen how successful we may be in presenting this new image of the Mysteries to the world. To this end I have written and lectured on the subject of "magic" in order that some of the distortions of the medieval days may be removed and the light of the ageless wisdom shine more clearly in these days of change and turmoil.

The continuity of family, social and national life has been disrupted by two great world wars, and the shadow of nuclear war hangs over all the world today. Under these conditions it is natural for many people to attempt to find stability by joining one or another of the arcane schools; particularly those schools which claim an ancient lineage. These fraternities, by their venerable ancestry, give to these people a feeling of security which they do not find in the outer world. This, however, is "escapism" and although we may withdraw from the world in this way, our only justification (apart from a relatively few special cases) is that in such a retreat we may contact energies which will enable us to resume the struggle with renewed vigour. It is well to remember, however, that "refreshment" follows upon "labour", and it is only those who have fulfilled their rightful service who receive their just dues.

In the new presentation of the esoteric philosophy this point is being strongly emphasized, for it is in what an initiate of the Mysteries *is,* rather than in what he *says,* that he really serves humanity. I believe the idea of the collective unconscious of the race, so carefully outlined by the psychologist C. G. Jung, to be a true concept, and, if we look at the esoteric schools from this standpoint, I think we can see how the initiate works. "No man is an island." Whether we talk of the "collective unconscious", or the *Anima Mundi,* or the "astral light", we are compelled to view each individual as being intrinsically linked with all his fellows, and indeed with all evolving life. Under these conditions he is constantly affecting, and being affected by, all other individuals and he lives in this great "group soul", if we may so describe it. One of the virtues of an esoteric school is that it forms a separate group within the greater group. Because it is linked with the collective unconscious on the one hand, and on the other is in touch with the collective superconsciousness (what the mystics have defined as the divine ground within the soul) its members are enabled to modify the tainted unconscious of the race by means of the divine energies which they can, and must, contact and direct if they are to be occultists in any real sense.

That this might be understood has been the underlying theme of all my writing, and will continue so to be in whatever I may write in the future.

"New Mansions for New Men." The age demands them and they will be built. However, it must also be remembered that the "mansions" referred to in Bible lore were the *mansioni,* the road stations of the Roman world, places where rest and refreshment could be obtained before one set out once more upon the way. In the end, it is eternally true that, as an Eastern saying (attributed to the Lord Jesus) has it: "This world is a Bridge; pass over it, but build no House thereon."

# BIBLIOGRAPHY

I AM not giving an extensive bibliography in connection with the subject of this book. The published books dealing with it fall into two main classes: those written to attack the philosophy of the Qabalah, and those written to defend it. The former are usually characterized by a pedantic dry-as-dust approach, and the latter by a credulous enthusiasm which defeats its own ends. A few books have appeared which were free from these distortions. These were, in the main, written by members of the esoteric fraternities. The first of these, in order of time and importance is, of course, *The Kabbalah Unveiled* by MacGregor Mathers. It is still in print, and although in many respects it needs revision, it is still a very useful book. The second book, which is still in print, is *The Mystical Kabbalah* by Dion Fortune, published by Williams & Norgate. This book contains the teaching which was received by those who were taught by Dion Fortune herself, and it is of the greatest value. Since its original publication, however, much water has passed under the bridges, and some of the teaching of *The Mystical Qabalah* is due for restatement. This has been done in two volumes entitled *A Practical Guide to Occult Symbolism* by Gareth Knight.

There are several other books on the Qabalah, but they are mostly written from the aloof intellectual angle, and are generally antagonistic to any esoteric ideas. For this reason I have not referred to them. Those who are interested can locate them through the usual channels.

The writings of Dr F. I. Regardie contain a very great deal of information on the Qabalah, as also do the four volumes of *The Golden Dawn*, published by the Aries Press, Chicago. These latter need to be read with discrimination, however.

A very interesting little book, *The Sepher Yetzirah*, by one of the founders of the Golden Dawn, the late Dr Wynn Westcott, is much deeper than its size suggests, and is best tackled after some preliminary work on more elementary expositions of the Qabalistic philosophy.

A word on esoteric publications may not be out of place here. They fall into three classes; those which are, in the main the results of direct personal experience on the part of their writers, those which are the result of much careful "scissors and paste" work, and which smell much more of the library atmosphere than the incense of the Lodge, and the greater numbers which are fiction of various grades. Cynics, of course, would lump the first and third classes together, and, indeed, much of what is claimed to be true teaching is so adulterated by the fictional element as to partially justify the critics.

A great deal of the material which has been regarded as the peculiar property of the "arcane" societies is, in point of fact, "public domain", as a series of visits to the British Museum Reading Room will prove. In this connection it may be noted that the word "arcane", which is applied to the esoteric fraternities, has the meaning of something deposited in a chest, and this is what has been done by very many esoteric brotherhoods. The available material has been treated as very, very secret, and doled out to the brethren as a special revelation. It is to the credit of the Society of the Inner Light, which was founded on a Golden Dawn contact by "Dion Fortune", that it has released much of its teaching for incorporation in Gareth Knight's two volumes. This includes not only the basic esoteric concepts, but the results obtained by their practice.

We are, as it were, working with a kaleidoscope, where, in addition to the usual number of coloured fragments, new pieces are introduced as the result of that working. The resultant patterns produced by this state of affairs are the justification for our practice. For all our writings are but as approximate symbols of that to which they point; they are indeed signposts on the way. By their use, we may make direct contact with the realities which now we perceive only "as in a glass, darkly", or, as the New English Bible has it, as "puzzling reflections in a mirror".

Many of us have been brought by vision and experience to the realization of the invisible concourse of forces; the field in which all life is working out its destiny, and it is with these forces and with Those who direct them that mankind, consciously or otherwise is directly concerned.

It remains to indicate some of the books which have been written on the subject of mysticism, and here I have decided to include works which are characteristic of both Christian and non-Christian mysticism.

Foremost in the list of books which deal with specific Christian mysticism are the works of that great Anglican writer Evelyn Underhill. Of these, the best is possibly her *Mysticism*. One who follows her very closely in point of value is Fr Poulaine, the Roman Catholic, whose book *The Graces of Interior Prayer* is of the greatest value to the student of the mystical tradition. That great work by Baron F. Von Hugel, who was one of the greatest of Roman Catholic lay theologians, *The Mystical Element in Religion*, as displayed in the lines of St Catherine of Genoa and her friends, is also a work of real value. We then come to *Studies in Mysticism* by A. E. Waite, a fine book, though marred somewhat by the peculiar style of its author. At the same time it ascends to the heights of poetic expression and, indeed, sublimity.

We now come to non-Christian mysticism, and one of the best, serving as a bridge between the two traditions is *Rational Mysticism* by W. Kingsland. Selections from the works of the Sufi mystic Jalah al-Din Rumi are to be found in one of the books entitled "The Wisdom of the East" series. It is a compilation by F. Hadland Davis. Another Sufi mystic, Al Ghazali is also included in "The Wisdom of the East" series of books. *The Secret of the Golden Flower,* a Chinese classic on the mystical life translated by Wilhelm and Jung, gives an excellent idea of one of the classic Chinese systems, whilst the various books on Zen Buddhism which are appearing at the present day will give a fair outline of basic Buddhist belief.

What is really required is a work which approaches this subject from a sympathetic but unbiased point of view, but for this I am afraid we shall have to wait for some time.